BRAIDED WIRE JEWELRY

Schiffer Publishing Ltd
77 Lower Valley Road, Atglen, PA 19310

Written, Illustrated and Photographed By
LORETTA HENRY

Acknowledgments

I would like to thank Arizona Gems and Minerals, Inc., for all their help and information. I would also like to thank my mother and father, Florence and Lawrence Tremblay, for always being there for me. Last but not least, my thanks to Demia and Damon Whittaker and Dahlia Hunter for their constant encouragement.

Printed in China

ISBN: 0-88740-867-2

Book Design By Audrey L. Whiteside

Henry, Loretta.
Braided wire jewelry / written, illustrated and photographed by Loretta Henry.
p. cm. -- (A Schiffer book for craftspeople)
ISBN 0-88740-867-2 (paper)
1. Jewelry making 2. Wire craft. I. Title. II. Series.
TT212.H454 1995
739.27'028--dc20 95-32218
CIP

Edited by Leslie Bockol

Published by Schiffer Publishing, Ltd.
77 Lower Valley Road
Atglen, PA 19310
Please write for a free catalog.
This book may be purchased from the publisher.
Please include $2.95 postage.
Try your bookstore first.

We are interested in hearing from authors with book ideas on related subjects.

Table of Contents

INTRODUCTION

Unlike many crafts or hobbies, braided wire jewelry doesn't require expensive tools or equipment and can be made by almost anyone. The most expensive tool necessary is a pair of smooth-jawed needle-nose craft pliers, which should cost about ten dollars. The other tools can usually be found around the house.

The semi-precious stones, beads, and wire can be purchased from rock (lapidary) shops and craft stores. The stones and beads come in a variety of shapes, sizes and colors. Wire also comes in different gauges (sizes), types, and shapes. The higher the gauge number, the thinner the wire. Types of wire range from gold and gold-filled to sterling silver, silver-plated, and copper. Wire can be purchased in a variety of shapes, such as round, half-round, and square. The square wire is very pretty when it is twisted. Braided wire jewelry looks delicate, but is actually quite sturdy. The watchband that is pictured in this book is one that I've been wearing every day for about two years.

Don't be afraid to experiment; get some cheap wire and try to make something original. In most of the projects that I have made, I have used silver and gold together to give contrast to the items that I was making, but this isn't necessary. What ever you make, make it your way!

Be sure to read the section of this book that deals with how to clean the jewelry, especially if precious or semi-precious stones and beads are used.

The diagrams in this book were not drawn to scale. They are meant for instructional purposes and not as exact replicas. In the diagrams for patterns that have frame beads on both outside wires, the beads were only shown on one side if the item was to be viewed from the side and not the front.

GOOD LUCK AND HAVE FUN!

BRAIDING TIPS

Holding the Wires

There's no right or wrong way to hold the wires while braiding. It's just a matter of what's comfortable for each individual. One secure way to hold the wires is to place the taped end in a pin-vise. Otherwise, simply hold the taped area with your thumb and finger, and use your other hand to braid the wires. I work from bottom to top, sliding the braided wire down between my thumb and finger as I braid.

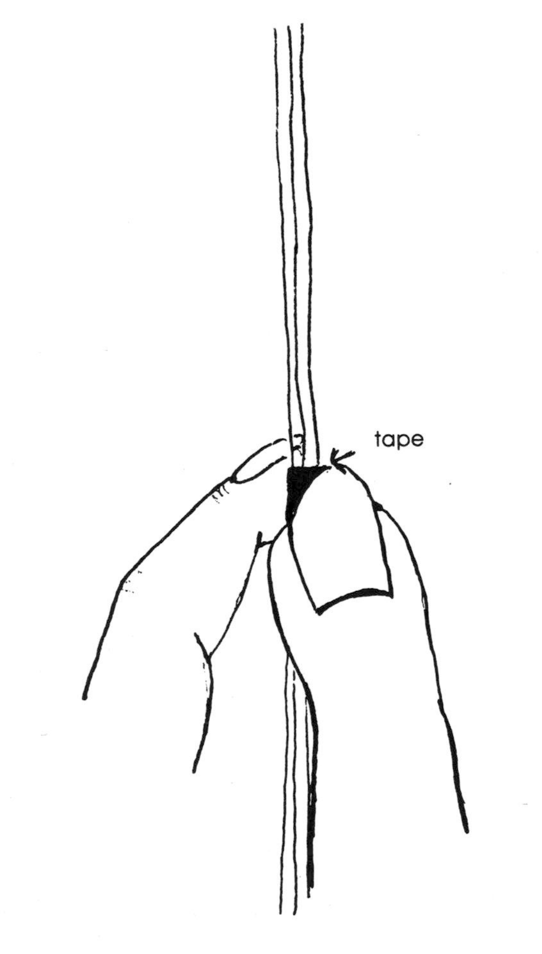

Starting the Braid

Starting the braid on the left and going to the right, the same way that we read, helps to keep your place in the pattern. When the first braid at the taped area is made, it sometimes looks as if the wires are not going to braid, but after the second braid it will start to look right; just continue braiding and follow the pattern. Bend the left outside wire over the center wire then the right outside wire over the center wire to make one complete braid. Try to make the braids tight and uniform.

Measuring

When measuring around a stone or your wrist to find the length that the wire will need to be cut for a stone frame, watch band or bracelet, keep in mind that approximately 3/16 inch of the wire per 1 inch length will be taken up by braiding. The amount of wire lost to braiding may change according to how tight or loose you braid. The chain loop will require about an extra 3/4 inch of wire.

Marking The Pattern

I use highlighters of several different colors to mark the pattern before I start braiding, which helps me to remember where I am in the pattern. As I start a paragraph I use one color to underline *x number of braids,* and a different color to underline *x number of beads and then braid,* and so on until the end of the paragraph. I find that this makes it easier to remember where I left off in the pattern, especially when there's a lot of repetition. Also, the highlighter will not damage or cover the pattern.

Cleaning Tips

Many precious and semi-precious stones can be damaged (if not completely ruined) when cleaned with ultra-sonic jewelry cleaners or commercial cleaning fluids. Opals, turquoise, jade, and emeralds, to name a few, should not be cleaned in commercial cleaning solutions. There are many more precious and semi-precious stones that can be harmed if cleaned improperly. You will need to check with your rock shop or jeweler to know which ones are at risk. If there is ever a question as to whether or not to clean a particular gemstone, a jeweler should be consulted.

Many of the solutions that are used to clean gold will cause silver to tarnish. A soft-bristled brush and toothpaste work very well on both metals. When the cleaning is finished, simply hold the jewelry under warm water and brush until the toothpaste is gone. Another way to clean your jewelry is to use a mild dish soap in place of toothpaste, as long as the dish soap *does not* contain ammonia or acids.

When cleaning a watchband it is not necessary to remove the band from the watchface. Hold the watch in your hand so that the face is covered. First clean one side of the band, and then the other side. Dry the band with a soft, dry cloth.

Project #1

HOOP EARRINGS

Hoops & Hearts with a Diagonal Bead Design

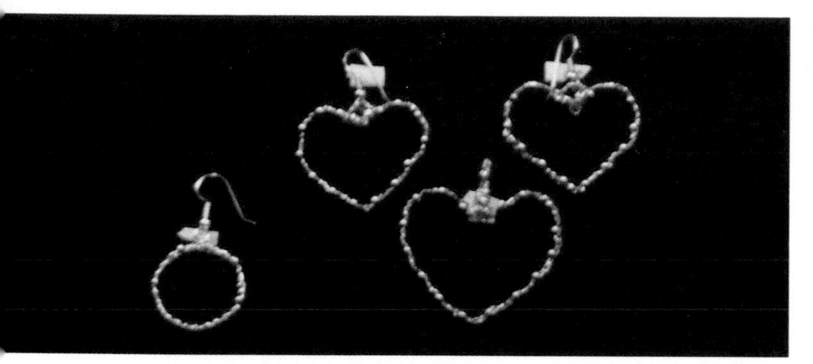

MATERIALS

24 gauge gold or silver wire
2 mm gold or silver beads (frame beads)

Gold and silver metal beads can be used in many different ways. In this book, they are referred to as 'frame beads' to avoid confusion with the stone beads used in other projects.

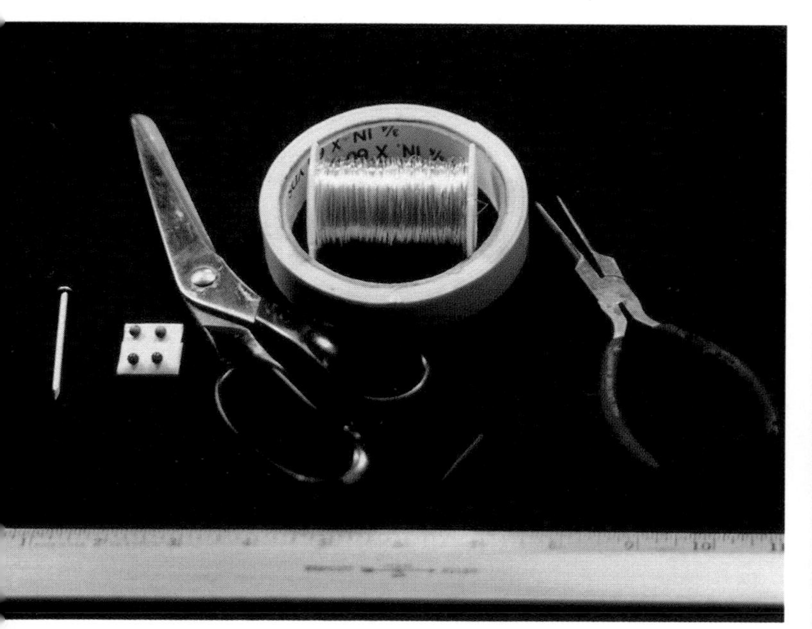

TOOLS

masking tape
craft pliers
nail
ruler
wire cutter or scissors

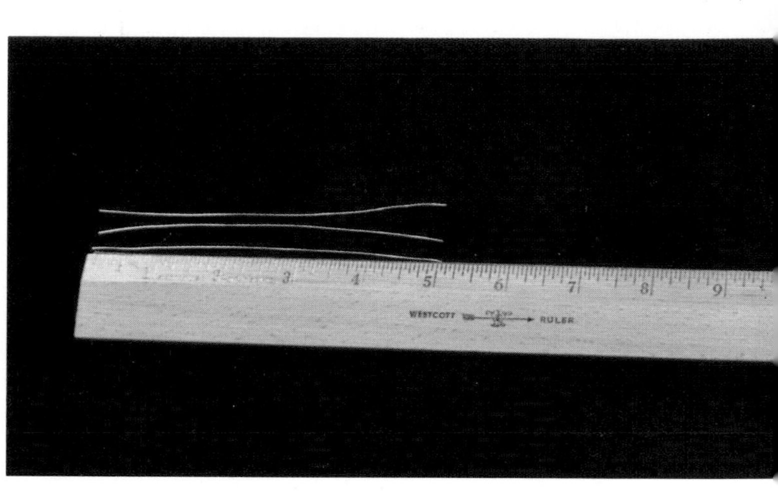

Each earring requires three wires. To make a pair, you will need to measure and cut six pieces of 24-gauge wire, each 5 inches long.

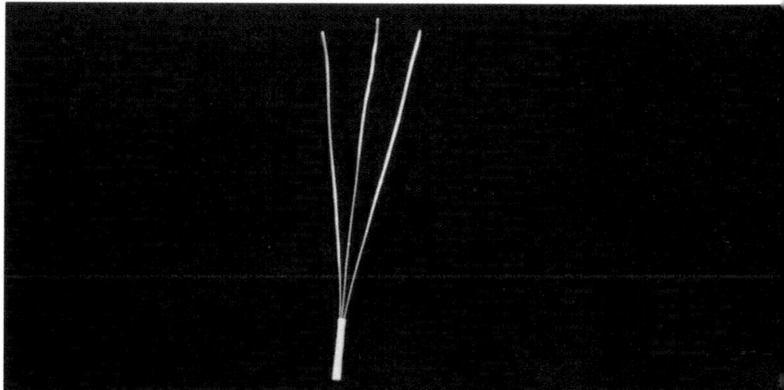

Hold three of the wires side by side, and tape them together at one end (fig. 1).

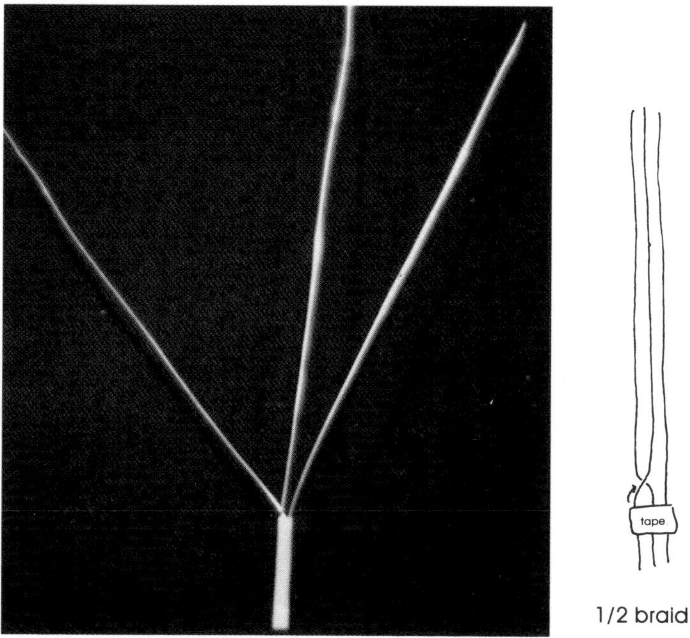

1/2 braid

(*) To start braiding, bend the left outside wire over the center wire, so that the left wire becomes the new center wire. This is *one-half of a braid.* As you work on this and other projects, try to make the braids uniform, not too loose and not too tight.

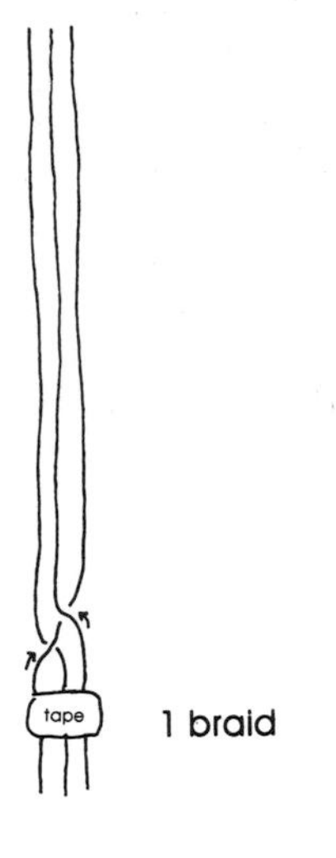

Next, bend the right outside wire over the center wire, so that the right wire becomes the new center wire. This makes *one complete braid.*

Repeat these two steps—bending the left outside wire over the center wire, then the right outside wire over the center wire—and *two complete braids* have been made.

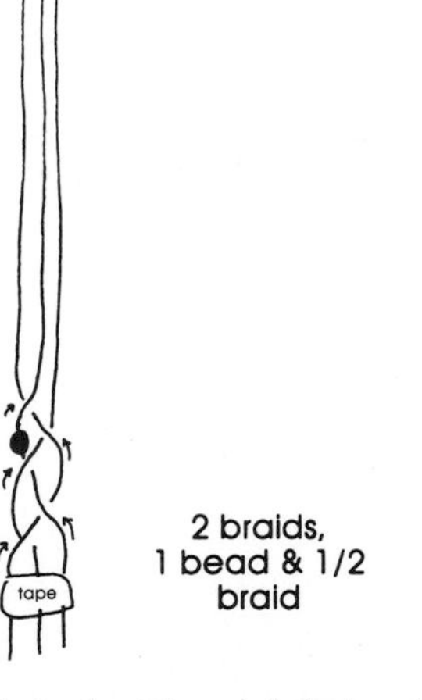

Now you can start adding beads in the Diagonal design. First slide one 2 mm frame bead onto the left outside wire. Then use your thumb to bend this wire over the center wire. Simultaneously, you can use your index finger to guide the old center wire to the left.

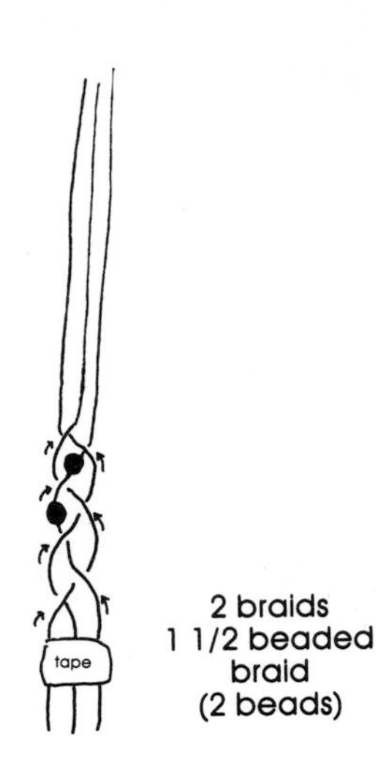

Put one frame bead on the new center wire, and then use your thumb to bend the right outside wire over the center wire. You can use your index finger to guide the center wire over to the right. Next, bend the left outside wire over the center wire.

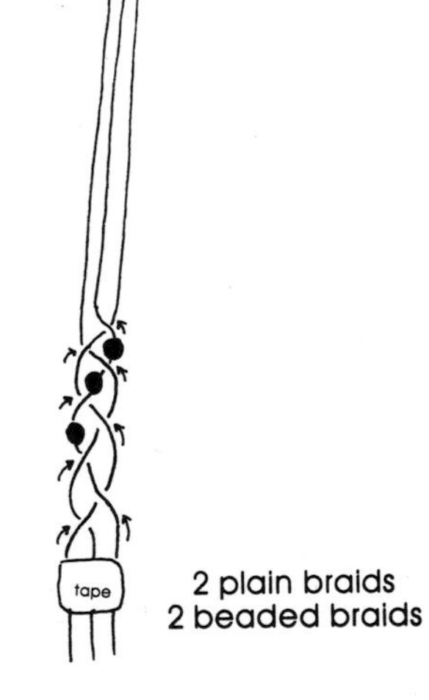

Put one frame bead on the right outside wire. Then use your thumb to bend the right outside wire over the center wire, guiding the center wire to the right with your index finger. This completes one set of Diagonal frame beads.

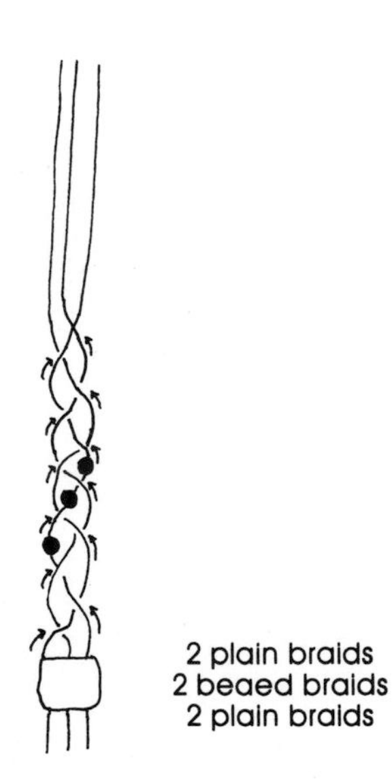

Follow the bead set by at least two plain braids.

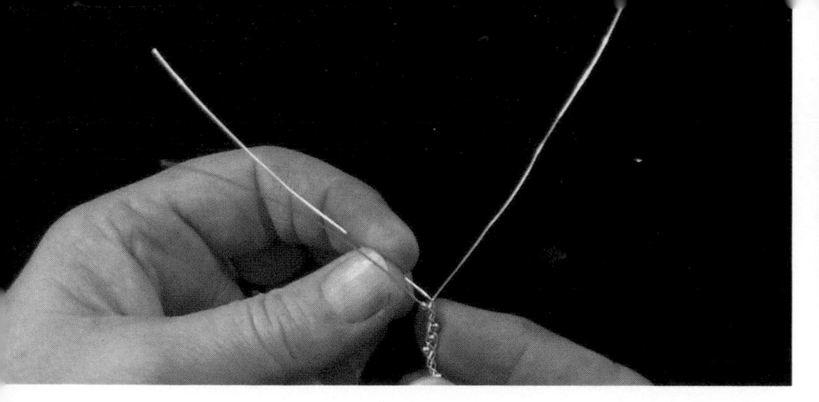

Repeat from the (*) above, alternating two plain braids with one set of Diagonal frame beads, until six sets of Diagonal frame beads have been made. In these photos you can see how I use my fingers to manipulate the wires and beads as I first put a bead onto the left wire...

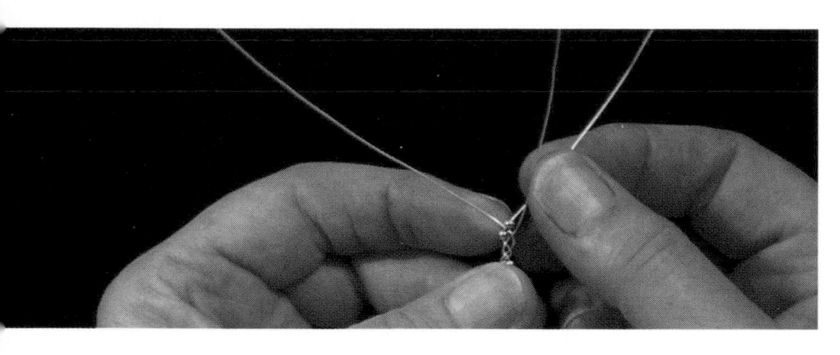

...then on the center wire...

...then on the right wire. After you've finished making six bead sets, continue to make plain braids down the remaining wire, to within 1/4 inch of the end. Remove the tape and all the adhesive residue.

To make the hoop, start bending the braided wire with your fingers to form a round loop.

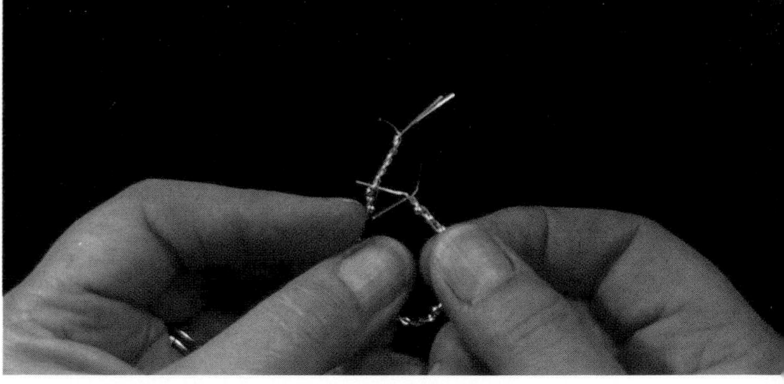

As the ends come together, pass the center wire of the end that had been taped through an opening just above the frame beads on the opposite side.

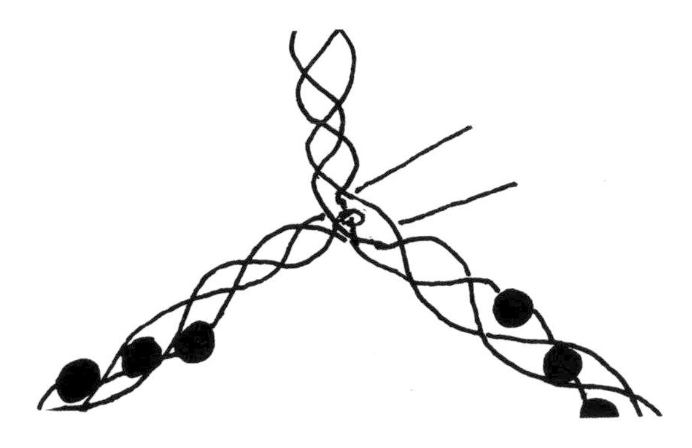

Bend this wire and pass it back through an adjacent opening in the braid. Then cut and tuck it out of sight.

Bend the unbeaded braided wire around a nail to form a small loop.

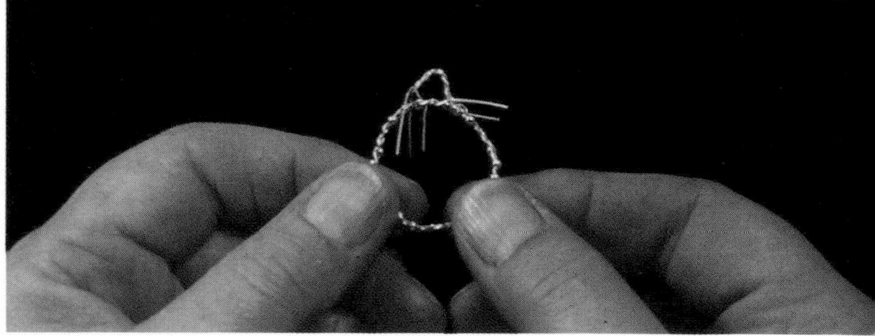

Separate the ends of the small loop's braid into three individual wires, and pass the center wire down through an opening in the hoop frame. Crimp the end of it to secure it in place, cut it if necessary, and tuck it out of sight.

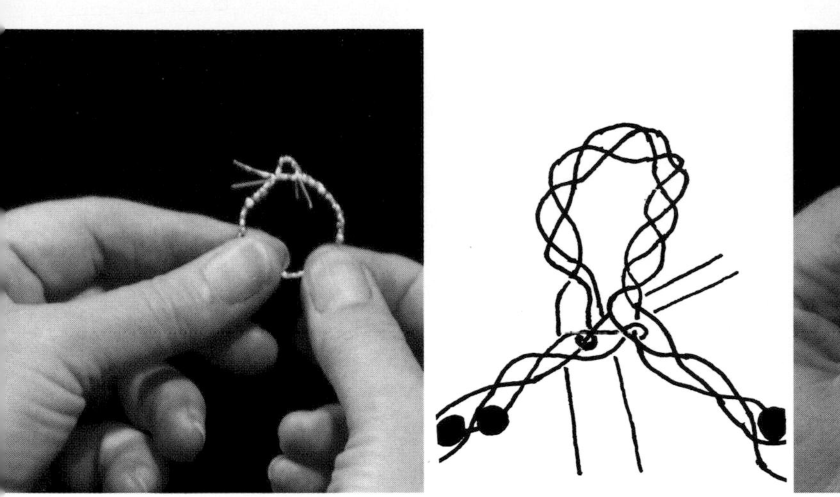

At this point there should be two wires facing down (from the small loop) and two wires facing out (from the frame hoop).

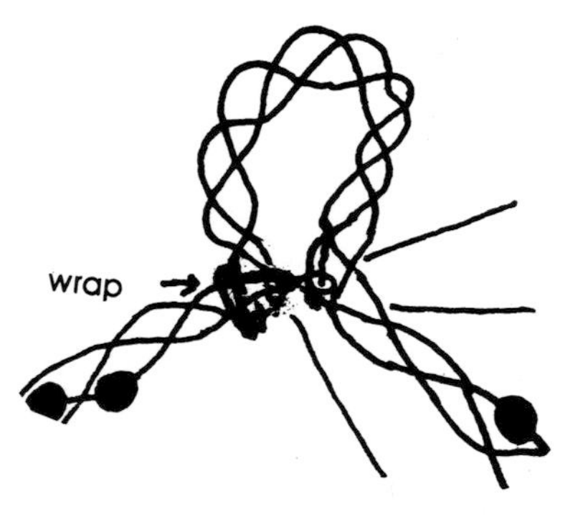

Take one of the wires that face down and wrap it around the hoop next to where the small top loop joins it.

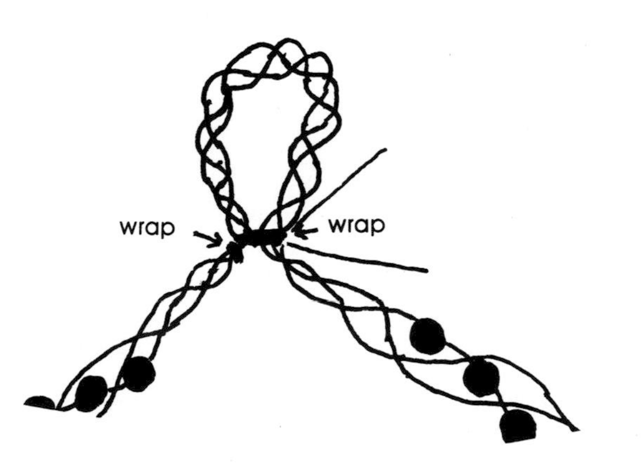

Now take the other wire and wrap it around the base of the small top loop where it joins the hoop.

Repeat this procedure with the wires that face out. Be sure that all the ends are tucked back into the braid, out of sight. After you make the second earring, the hoops can be put onto pre-made, commercially-purchased earring wires, posts, or clip earrings. Follow the same instructions to make a necklace pendant, but cut your wires to be 6 inches long instead of 5 inches, and use eight sets of beads instead of just six; in addition, you will have to give the loop at the top a half-turn so the neckchain can pass through.

This same pattern can be used to make heart-shaped earrings and necklace pendants. After the hoops are made, find the center of the hoop's bottom and bend it to a point. Now push the chain loop down toward the center of the hoop. This should form a heart, but you may need to use your fingers to complete the shaping. On the piece shown in this diagram, the loop has been given a half-turn so that the piece can be hung from a neckchain.

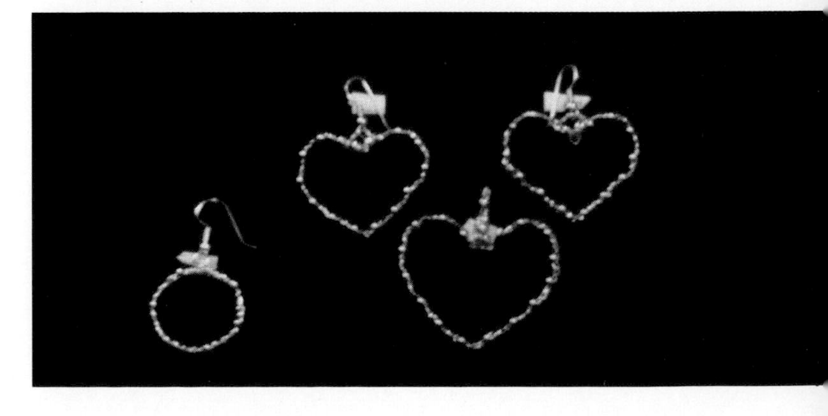

Here are some hoop-shaped and heart-shaped pieces, fitted as earrings and a pendant.

Project #2

BRAIDED WIRE FRAMES

MATERIALS

22 gauge or 24 gauge gold or silver wire.
frame beads (optional)
wires
gemstones
neckchain, earring wires, or pinback

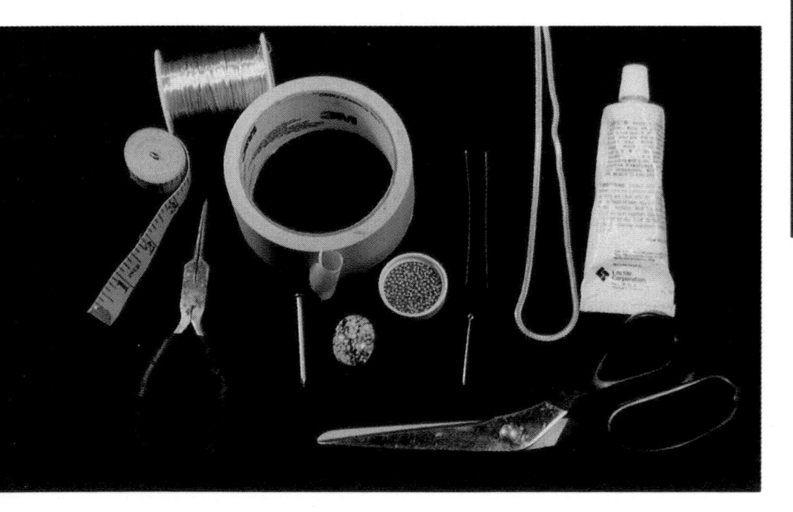

TOOLS

dressmaker's cloth tape measure
smooth-jawed needle-nose pliers
Epoxy glue
pin or needle
nail

Braiding the Frame

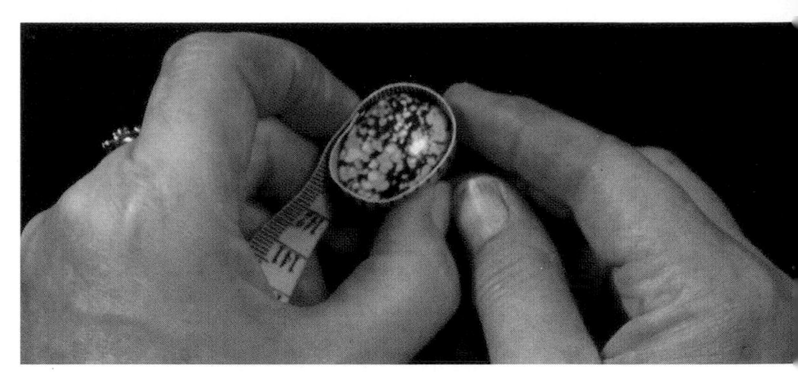

Lay the stone on a flat surface and measure around it with the dressmaker's tape measure. Be sure to measure *around* the stone, not *across* it. Measuring around the stone will tell you how much braided wire you will need to frame the stone. If frame beads are added to the frame, they will take up a little extra wire. Also, the neckchain loop has to be allowed for. Usually 3/4 inch to 1 inch will give enough unbraided length for the chain loop.

The stone that is pictured in this book measures 3 inches around the outside. To that measurement, 1 inch was added for the neckchain loop and the loop wrap. Another 1/2 inch was added to allow for the double-sided frame beads and braiding of the wire. The total amount of 24 gauge wire was three pieces, each 4 1/2-inches long.

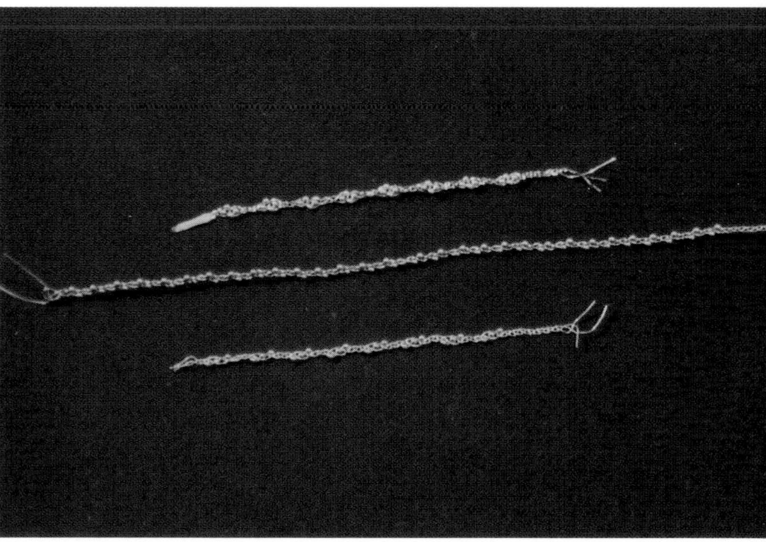

Before you measure out and cut any wire for this project, you have to decide if you want to use frame beads or just a plain braid. Too many frame beads can detract from the beauty of the stone, but frame beads done right can really enhance your piece.

The Diagonal and the Diamond frame bead designs look best when at least two plain braids are braided between sets of beads, thus averaging two sets of 2 mm beads per inch. This measurement includes two plain braids, one bead set, two plain braids, and one bead set, ending the wires with another two plain braids at the end. The Double-Sided frame bead pattern should have a least two plain braids between bead sets.

These measurements may vary according to how tight or loose you braid. In addition, the size of the bead can make a difference as to how many beads there are per inch. The best way to determine how many beads there are per inch (according to the tightness of your own braiding) is to braid the beads onto some inexpensive wire and then measure the wire. My suggestion is that you buy some inexpensive craft wire in different gauges for practice. Cut three 6-inch pieces of each gauge and braid them one at a time, both with and without bead patterns. Then measure the finished braid of each gauge and pattern and mark down the results from each. For example,

Gauge	Unbraided	Braided	Bead Design
24	11 inches	10 inches	Double-Sided
"	6 inches	5 1/2 inches	Diagonal
"	6 inches	5 1/2 inches	Diamond

Shown here, from top to bottom, are braids in the Diamond bead design, the Double-Sided bead design, and the Diagonal bead design. The heavier 22 gauge wire will take a little more unbraided wire. If you spend some time experimenting this way, you will be able to estimate how much wire is needed for many other projects you may try in the future. In the back of this book there is a worksheet (much like the chart here) for this purpose.

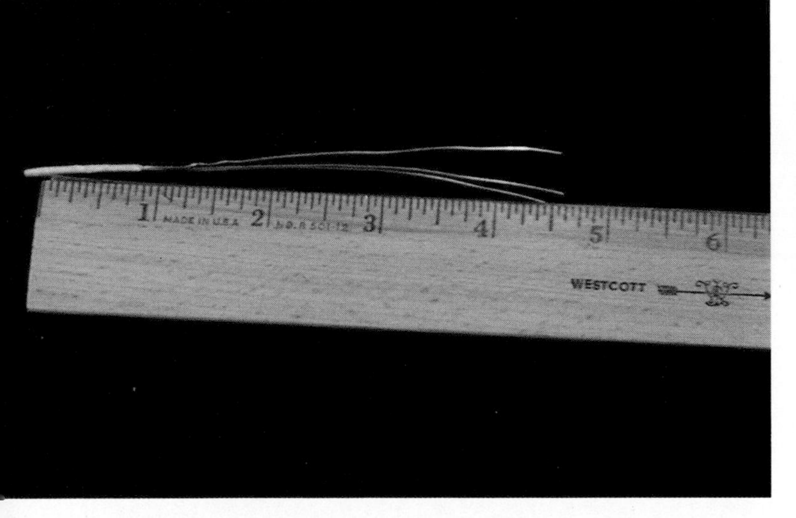

After the length for the unbraided wire has been determined, measure and cut three wires. Hold the wires together, touching with the ends even, and tape the wires together about 1 inch from the end.

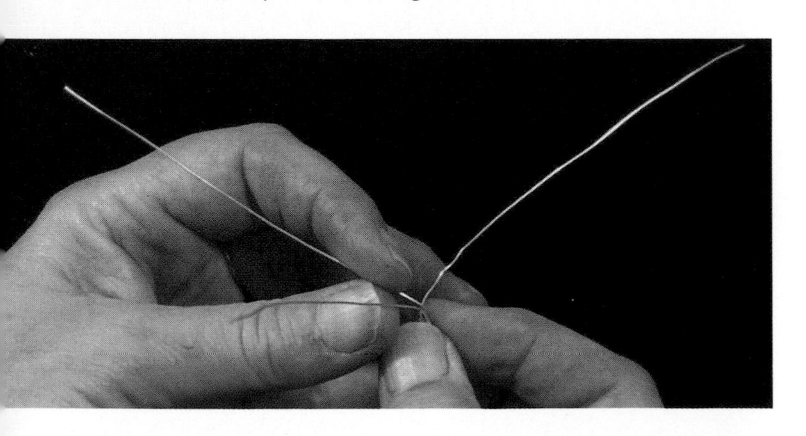

Start braiding at the tape using a bead design or a plain braid to make the frame for your stone. Beginning from the taped segment, make two plain braids. Then, if you have decided to use a bead design, start placing the beads on the wire (see pp. 5-6 for an explanation of plain braids, and see the glossary for explanations of several different bead designs).

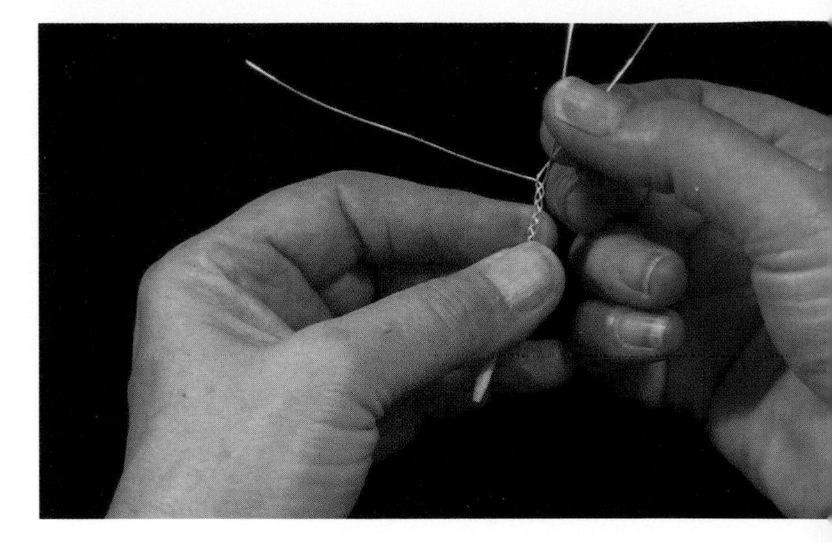

Continue the plain or beaded pattern until about 3/8 inch from the end to complete the stone frame braid. Then remove the tape and rub all the adhesive from the other end of the braided wire. Braid just a bit more (without beads) to allow for the chain loop, until about 1/4 inch of unbraided wire remains.

Bend the braided wire around the stone with the ends of the wire at the top of the stone. Bring the sides together to make a tight frame.

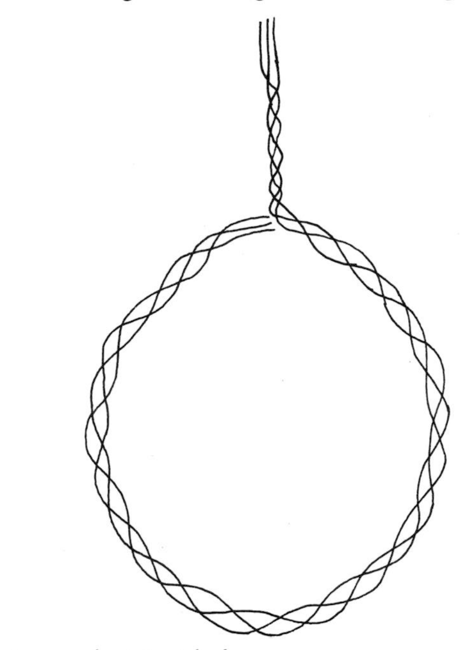

Remove the stone and set it aside for now.

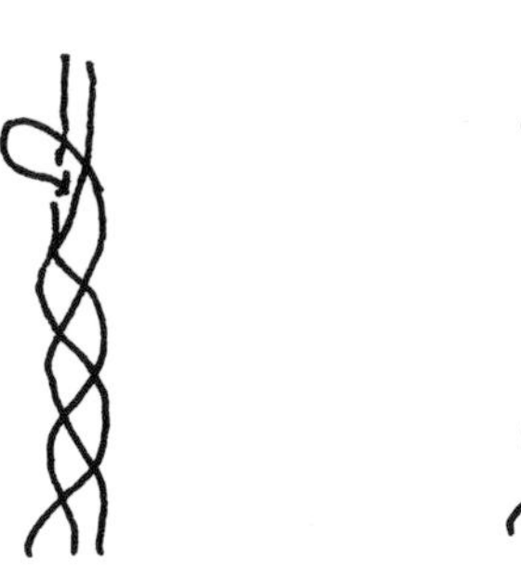

To make a finished-looking piece, you need to make sure all stray wires are cut short and tucked neatly back into the piece. Here, for example, there are three loose wires at the end of the braided frame (at 12 o'clock). First cut one of the outside wires, and then tuck it back into the braid securely.

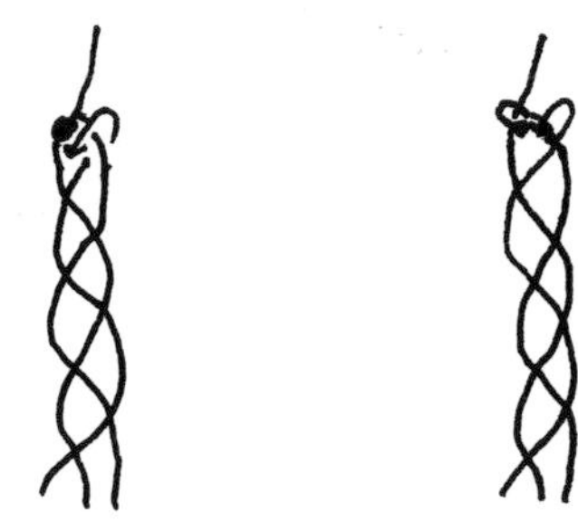

Then do the same with the second outside wire.

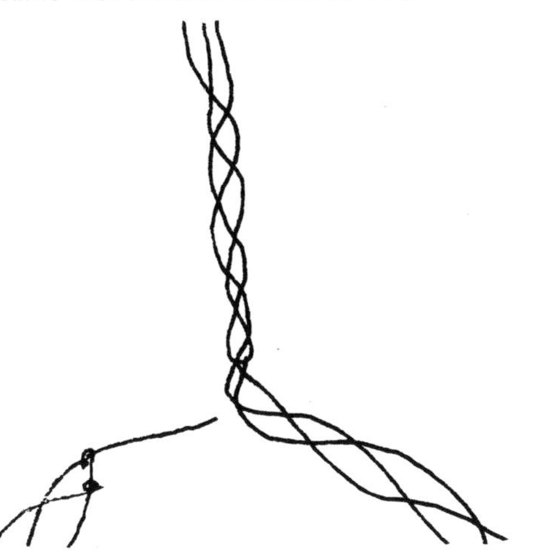

You should now be left with only the single center wire sticking out.

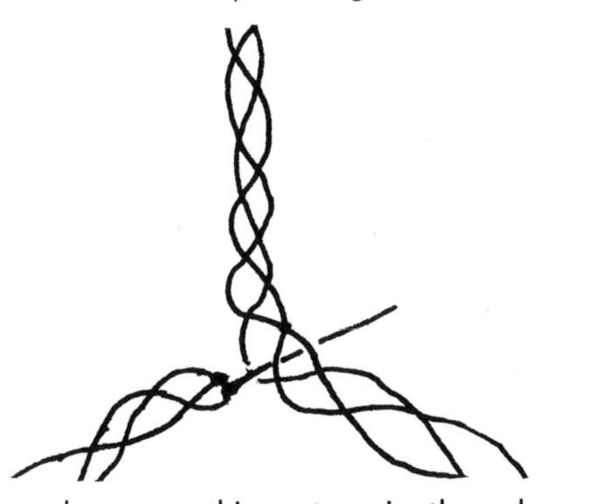

To close the frame loop, pass this center wire through an opening at the base of the neckchain loop braid. If you are not sure which opening to use, put the stone back into the frame, press the frame wire snug around it, and pass the single wire through the opening just above the top of the stone.

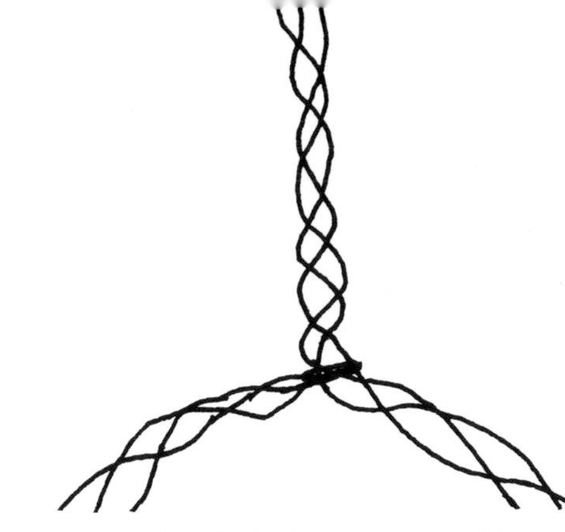

Pull the wire snug so that the braids from both sides are touching. Push the end of the wire back through another opening, cut the wire if it is too long, and tuck it out of sight.

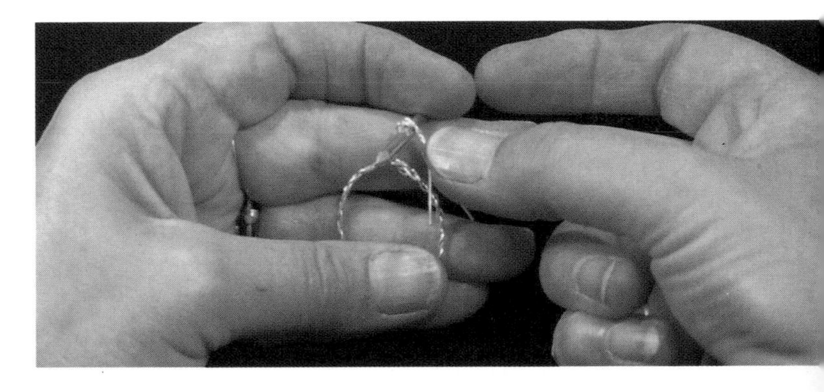

To make the neckchain loop, roll the remaining loose braid over a nail to form a circle.

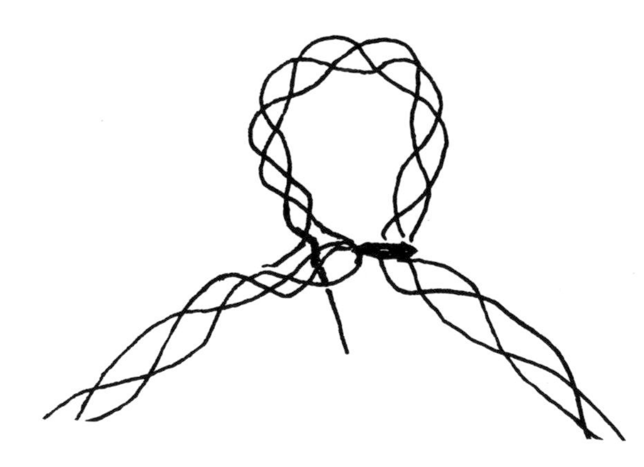

Push the center wire of the neckchain loop down through an opening in the top of the frame.

I use the needle-nose pliers to pull it tight.

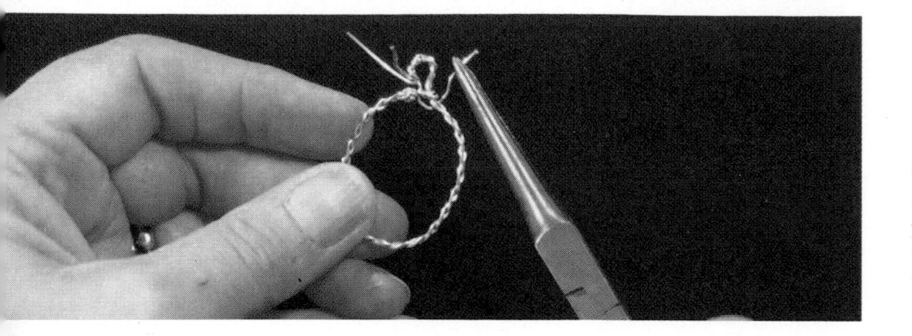

Then push it back up through another opening.

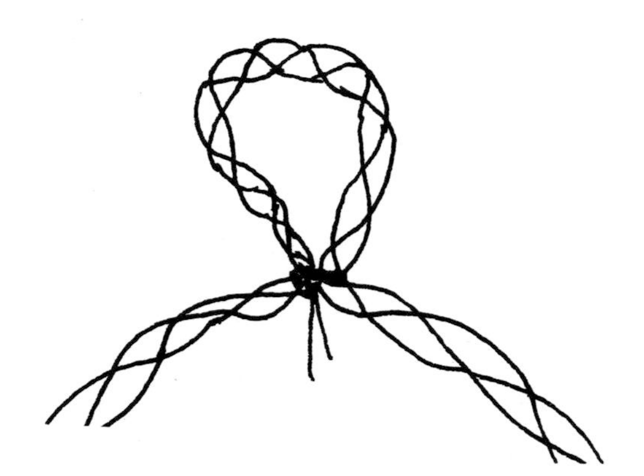

Next, wrap the center wire once around the top of the stone frame, cut if necessary, and tuck it out of sight. The two outside wires should still be loose.

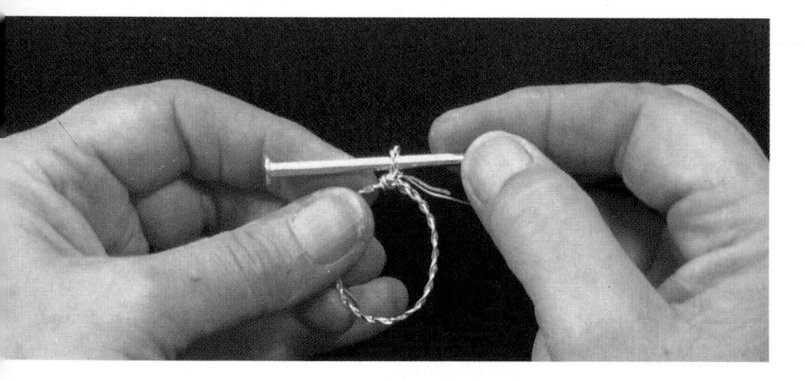

Hold the frame firmly between your thumb and fingers, and twist the neckchain loop a half-turn with the pliers or the nail. Cut one of the two remaining wires and tuck it out of sight.

Then wrap the last wire around the base of the chain loop twice and tuck it out of sight, cutting the wire if it is too long. Put the stone back in the frame.

Making the Retaining Wires

Retaining wires hold the stone in place. They can be made in many ways. The simplest style of retaining wire is made from the same type of wire as was used to braid the frame. Cut two pieces of this wire, each twice the length of the stone plus 3/8 inch.

Make a crimp in one end of each wire to form a hook. (*) Push the straight end of one wire through an opening at the base of the frame, going up over the face of the stone. The retainers need to be vertical, running up the right- and left-hand sides of the stone. Here I am working on the right-hand retaining wire first.

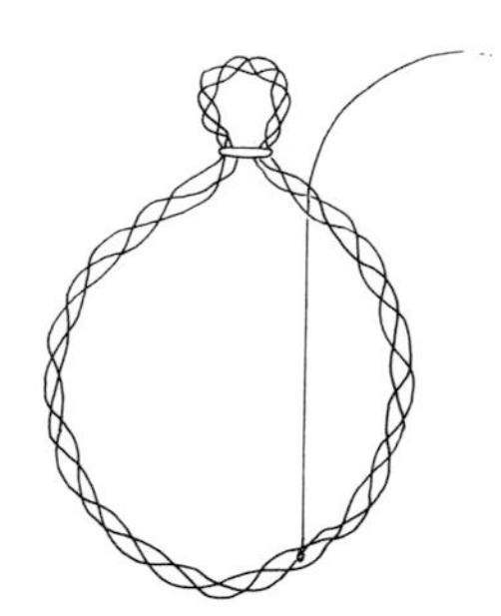

Next, push the wire out an opening at the top, staying on the right-hand side. Close the hook at the bottom of the stone frame where you started.

Take hold of the wire that is sticking out of the top of the frame. Bend it and push it through another opening at the top of the frame, so that it is sticking out at the back of the stone.

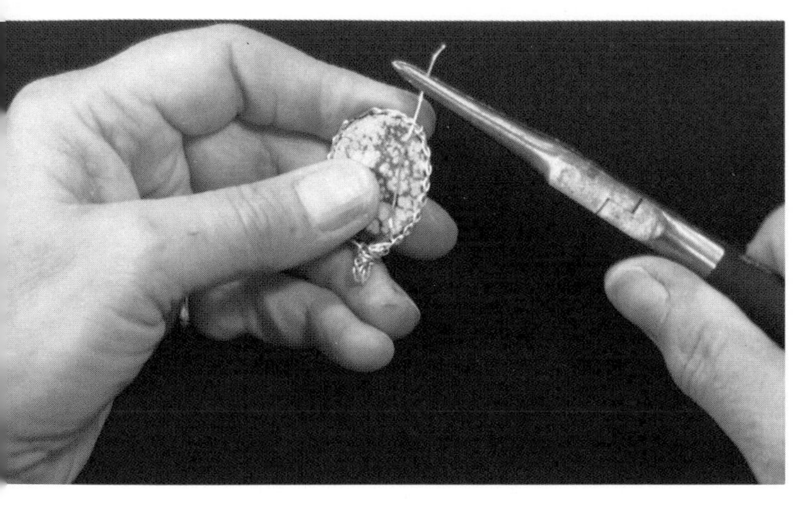

Then run the wire down the back of the stone, and push it out an opening at the bottom of the frame.

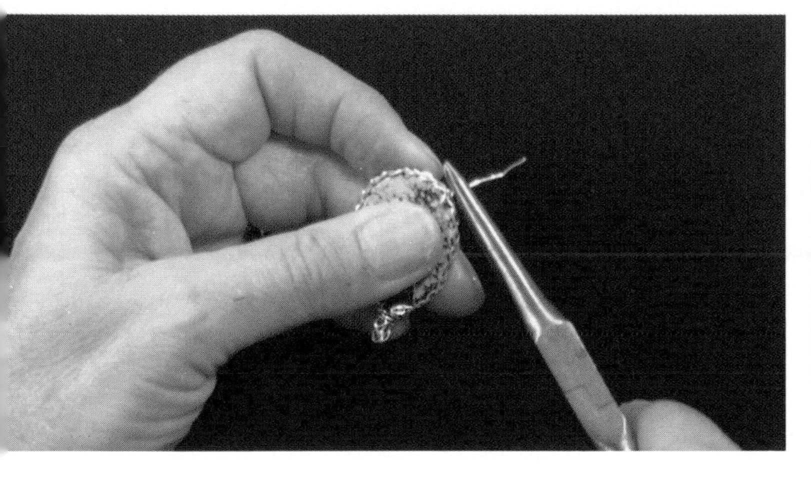

Bend the end of the wire and tuck the tail of it back into another opening so that it is out of sight, cutting if necessary.

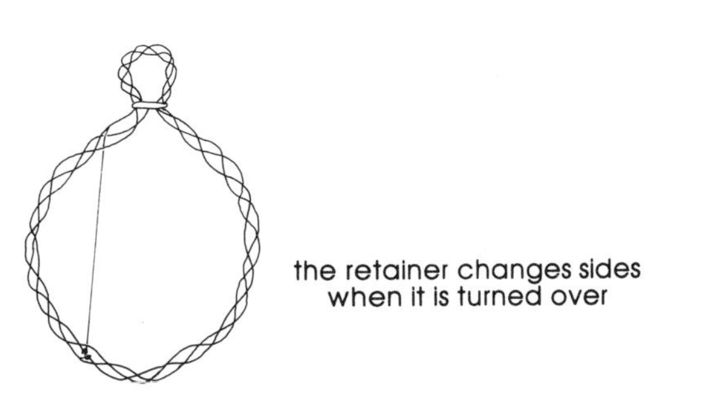

If you push it through an opening right next to the one you started with, the retainer on the back of the stone will match the retainer on the front of the stone perfectly. This diagram shows the view of the frame's back. The only difference between the front and back views of the finished retaining wire is that it seems to switch sides!

Repeat this process, starting from the (*) above, to make the retainer on the left hand side.

Retaining Wires: another style

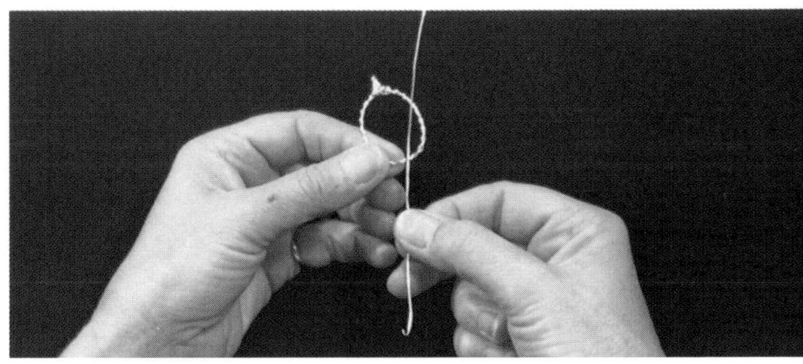

Another style of retainer is actually one continuous wire. Multiply the length of the stone by 4, and then add 1/2 to 3/4 inch to the total. Cut a segment of this length from the same wire you used to make the braided frame. Make a hook at the end of the wire, and then push the other end through an opening at the base of the frame (at 6 o'clock). Do not crimp the wire closed at this time.

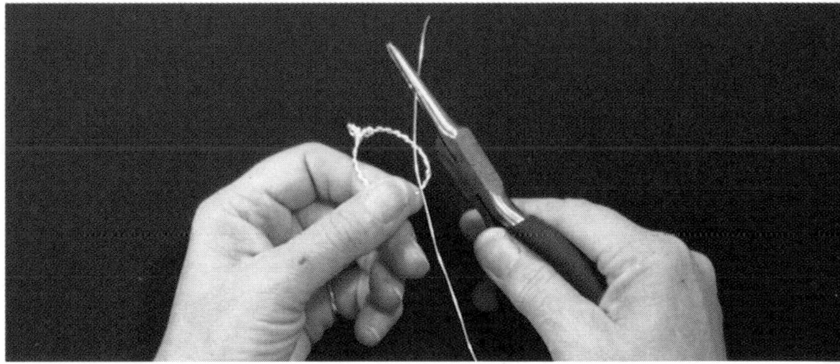

From there, angle the wire halfway up the side of the frame, and push the end through another opening (at 3 o'clock). Pull it through using your needle-nose pliers.

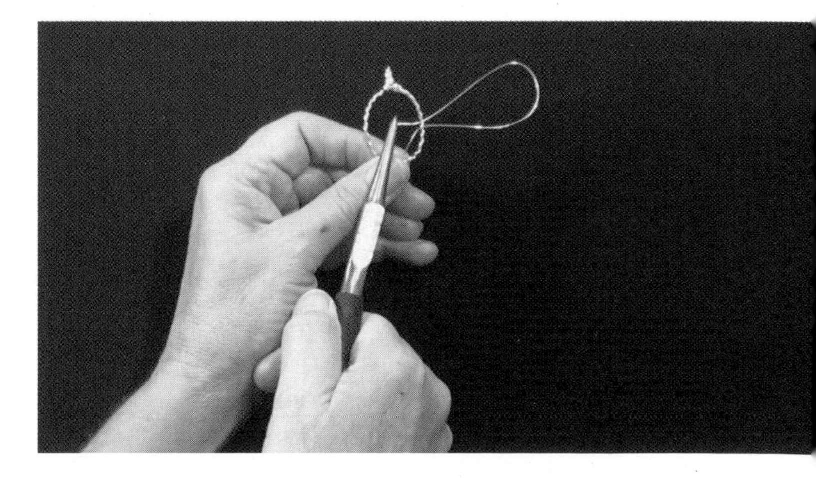

Tnread the wire back through an adjacent opening, and angle it towards the center top of the frame (at 12 o'clock). Run the wire in through one opening there, back out, and across to the other side of the frame (9 o'clock). Thread it in through one opening there, and back out. Pull it over to the six o'clock position, and run it through the hook that was left open. Then crimp the hook closed.

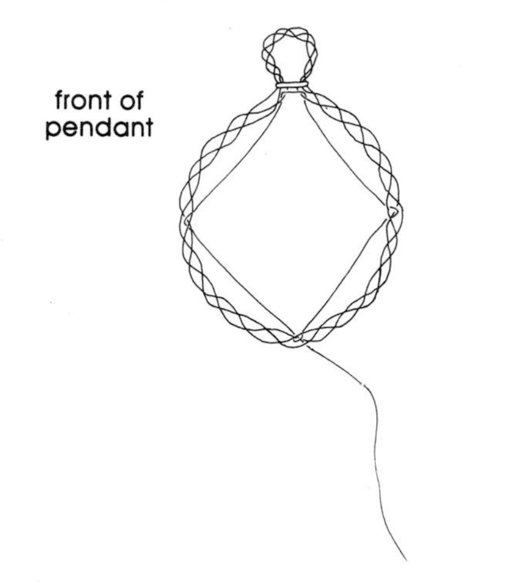

This will make a pattern of four diagonal retaining wires on the front of the stone.

Notice that there is still a lot of extra wire dangling from the bottom.

The longer wire can now be used (following the same instructions) to make four identical retainers on the reverse side of the stone.

Thread the wire in and out of openings at 3 o'clock, 12 o'clock, 9 o'clock, and back down to 6 o'clock.

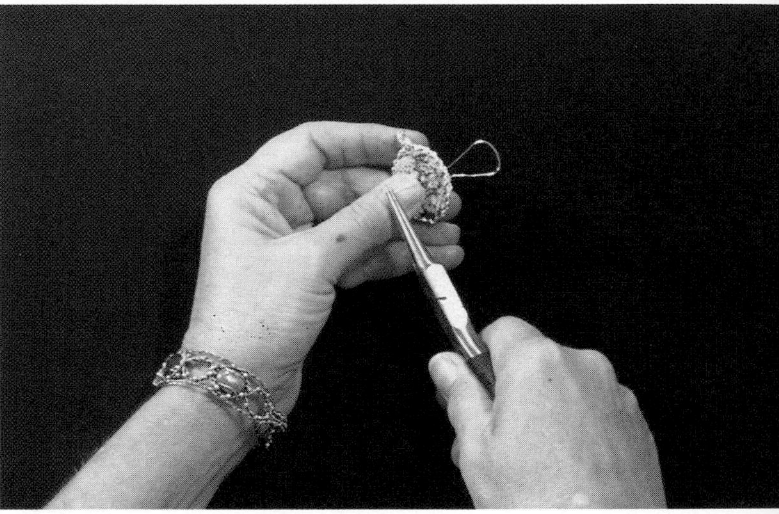

When you reach the end of the retainer at the back, push the end of the wire under and wrap around the same wire that the other end was wrapped around and tuck the end to the inside of the frame.

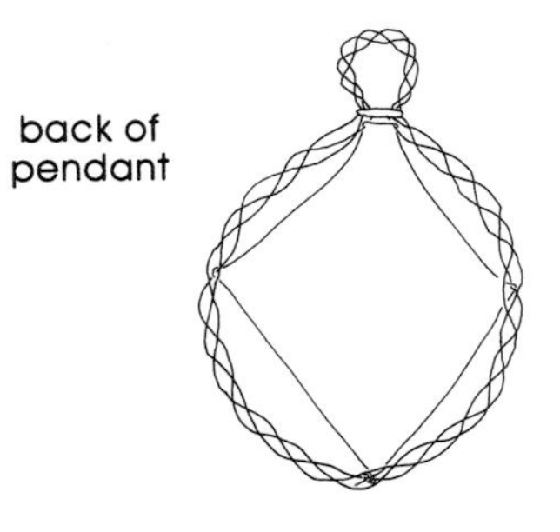

When all the ends are neatly tucked away, the retainers are finished!

The application of Epoxy Glue is optional. I like to place a very small amount on the wires that have been tucked and on the retaining wires where they cross the back of the stone.

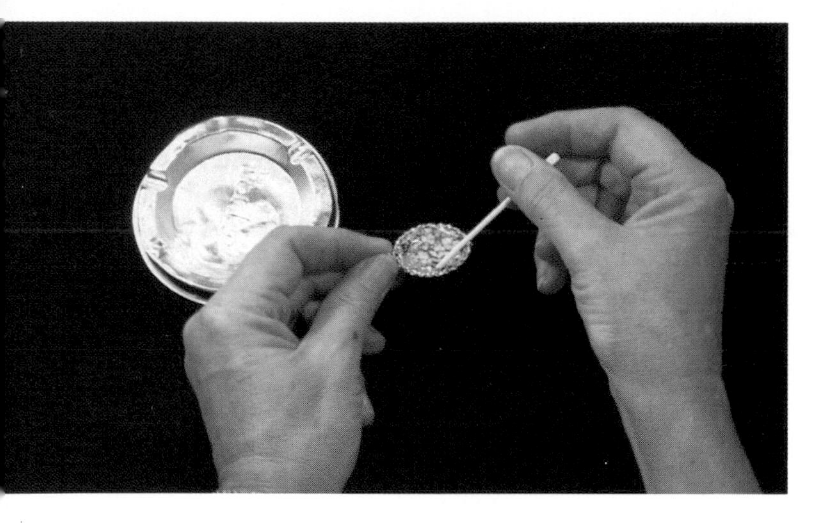

Mix a very small amount of the Epoxy glue and use the point of a needle, pin, or toothpick to apply it to the stone frame. Let the jewelry dry for 24 to 48 hours before handling it.

Adding Curlicues

One way to add extra interest to your pieces is to make wire decorations like curlicues on the edges of the stone. To make curlicues on a piece with the simple type of (two) retaining wires, begin with the first newly-cut retaining wire. Instead of putting a crimped hook at the end, leave an extra 1/2 inch dangling at the base of the stone frame. Then run the wire through the top and over the back. Secure the back wire by pushing it through the frame and hooking it over a frame wire and the dangling wire. Now using the tips of the pliers, roll the end of the dangling wire around them. Remove the pliers and push the wire curlicue against the stone. Try to center it.

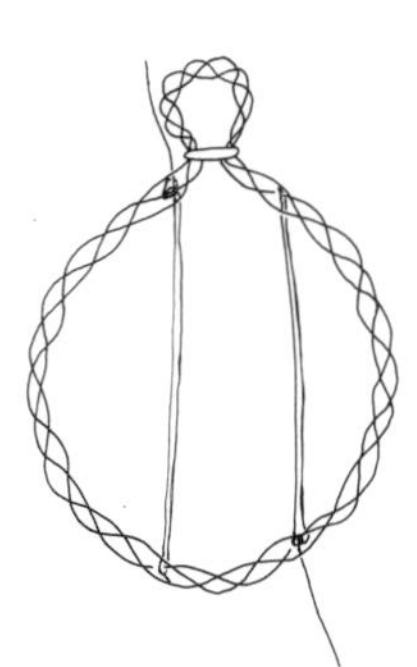

If you start the second retaining wire at the bottom, too, you will end up with two curlicues at the bottom of the frame, and none at the top. To get a curlicue at the top and one at the bottom, you will need to start threading the second retaining wire at the top, instead of at the bottom. Again, leave 1/2 inch of wire at the start (instead of making a crimped hook). Run the wire down to the bottom, thread it in and out of the braided frame, and then bring it back up to the top.

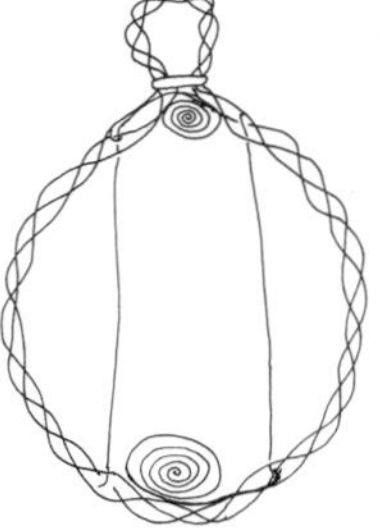

Make the top curlicue just as you made the bottom one.

With minor adjustments, you can make curlicues to decorate a frame with the more complicated style of retaining wires, as in this finished frame for an opal.

Here are some finished frames.

Project #3

DREAM CATCHER

Earrings & Necklace Pendant

It is an Indian belief that both good and bad dreams are caught in the webs of dream catchers like these. The bad dreams are burned up in the sunlight and only the good dreams remain to be dreamed again.

Materials
(for two earrings and one necklace)

two medium braided wire hoops
one large braided wire hoop
32 turquoise beads
18 garnet beads
two yards gold or silver lamé thread
15 pieces of 22 gauge silver or gold wire, each 1 1/2 inches long, *or* 15 eye pins
15 jump rings
15 small feather charms *or* 15 cheek bones
2 fishhook earring wires
18-inch gold or silver neckchain

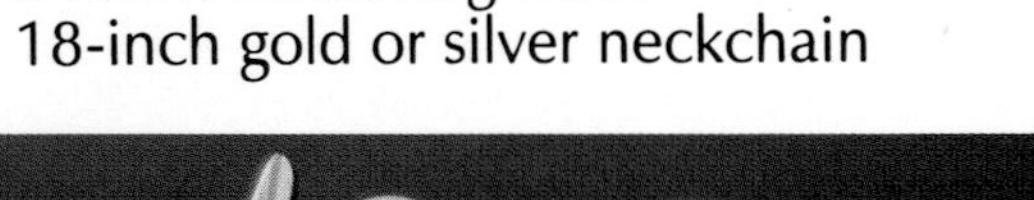

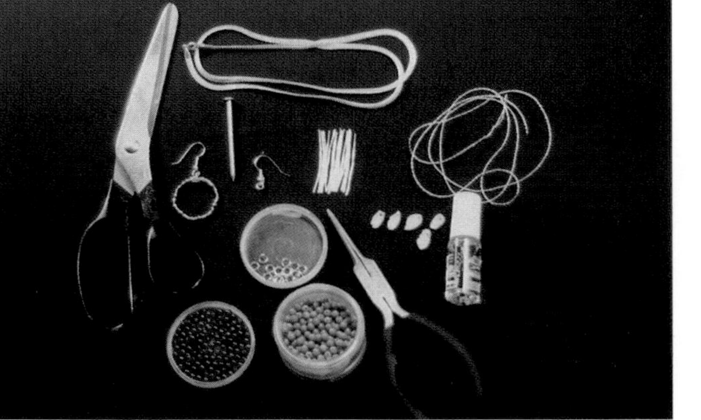

Tools

scissors
glue or clear nail polish
craft pliers
medium-size nail

To make an earring, start with a medium-size hoop about 1 inch across. Cut an 18-inch length of the lamé thread to make the web. Tie one end of the thread to the center of the hoop at the top.

At about 1/4 to 1/2 inch from the tie, push the thread through an opening in the braided hoop and back through the next opening. Pass the end of the thread between the thread and the braided frame. This makes a half hitch knot.

Go another 1/4 to 1/2 inch and make the next half hitch knot. Keep the thread snug, but be careful not to break the thread. While making the next knot, hold the previous knot with two fingers to keep the thread from slipping.

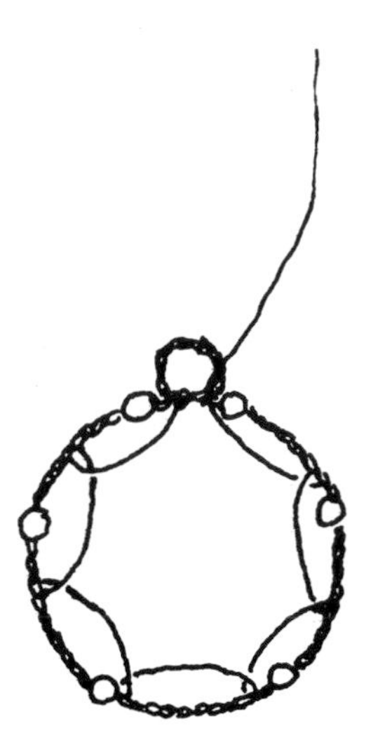

Continue around the hoop until you get back to the start.

String a turquoise bead on the thread and make a half hitch knot in the center of the first stretch of lamé thread.

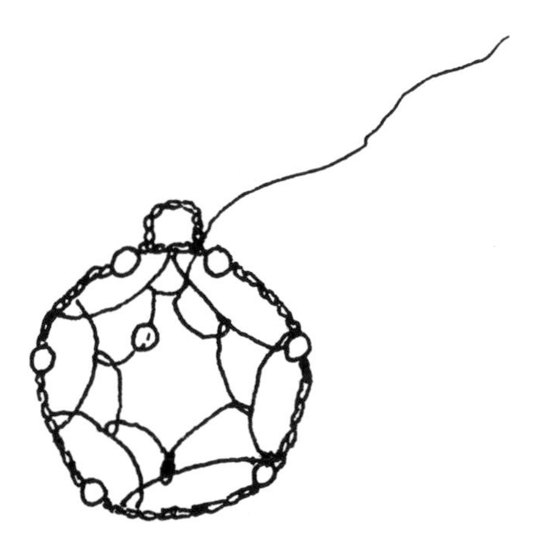

Make a half hitch knot in the center of the next half hitch knot segment of lamé thread and repeat until you are almost to the center. String a garnet bead on the thread and continue making half hitch knots until the center opening is the desired size.

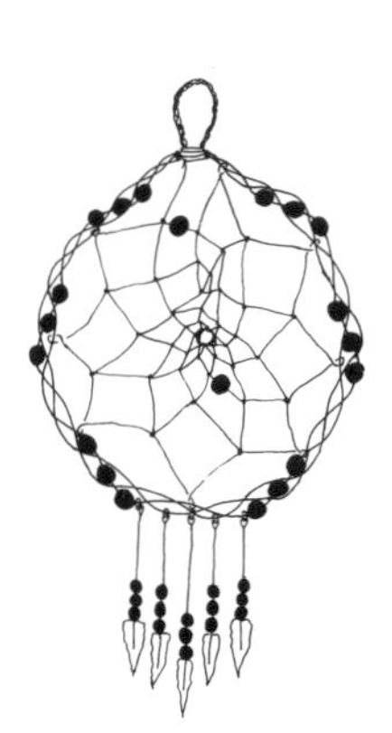

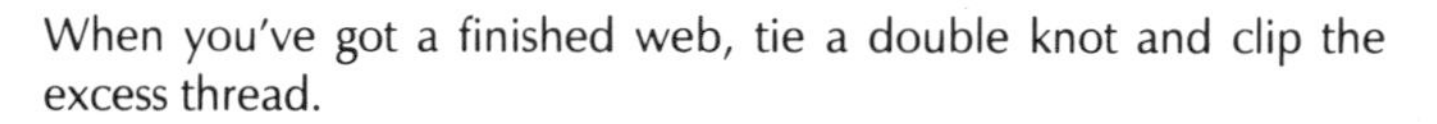

When you've got a finished web, tie a double knot and clip the excess thread.

If you prefer, a tiny drop of glue (or clear nail polish) about the size of a pinhead can be used to secure the ends of the beginning and the ending knots. Here I am painting clear nail polish over each of the half hitch knots to protect them and hold them securely.

When the glue or polish is dry, attach the earring hanger to the top of the hoop.

Then attach five jump rings to the bottom of the hoop, one at the center, and two on each side at equal distances.

Put one beaded eyepin on each of the 5 jump rings. Make sure that the eye at the bottom faces the same direction as the eye at the top.

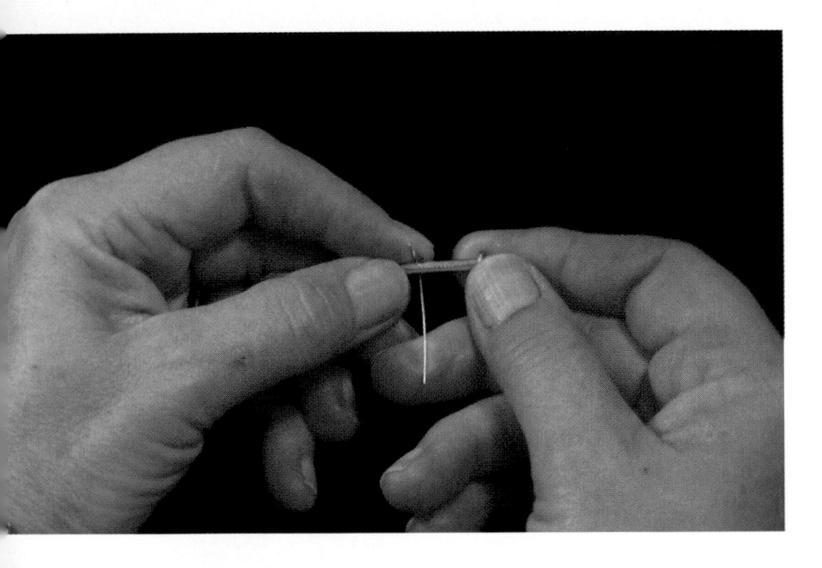

To make the eyepins that are used for the dangles, roll one end of each 1 1/2-inch piece of wire around a medium sized nail until an eye is formed (fig. 2).

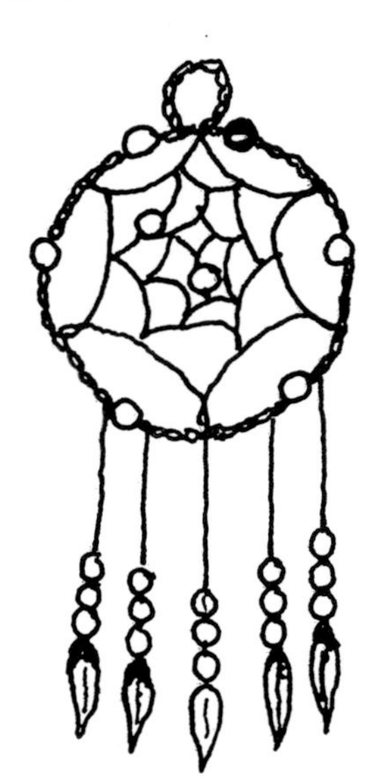

If you are using a feather charm, let the charm drop down into the loop of the eye and close the eye around it.

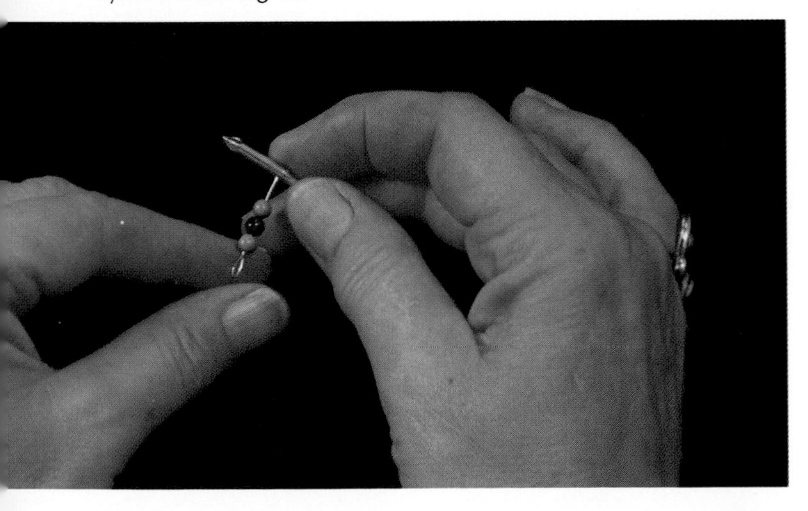

Next, thread a turquoise bead, a garnet bead, and another turquoise bead onto the wire of the eyepins. You can also add a feather charm if you'd like. To secure them, roll the bottom of the wire around a medium sized nail to form another eye.

Use this basic method to make the second earring. To make the pendant necklace, only a few minor changes are needed: first, use a larger hoop; second, cut a longer length of lamé thread (about 24 inches); and third, make a half-turn in the neckchain loop so that the chain can pass through it smoothly and the pendant can lay flat, as with the heart and hoop pendants explained earlier.

Project #4

BEADED CROSS

A Pendant

MATERIALS

24 gauge sterling silver or gold wire
approximately 60 gold or sterling silver beads
(3 mm for frame beads)
four 4 mm stone beads
one 6 mm stone beads
22 gauge gold or silver wire for wrapping
28 gauge wire for stringing beads

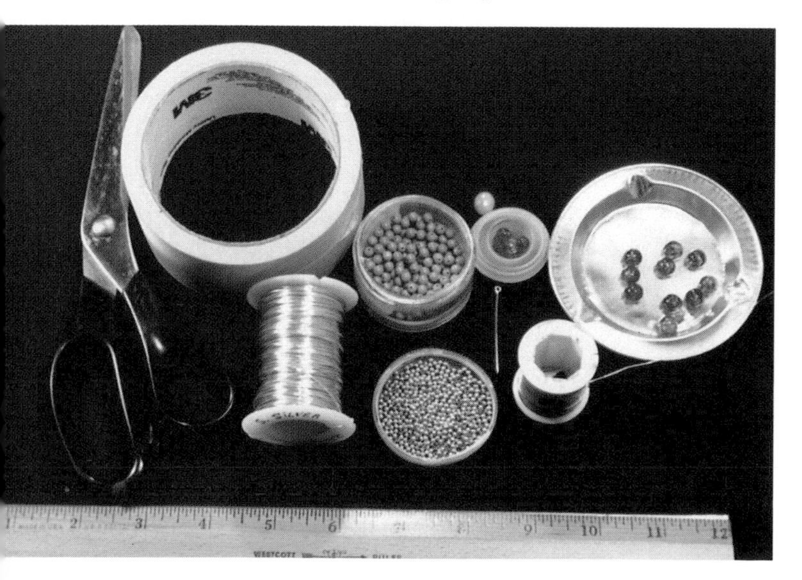

TOOLS

masking tape
needle or small pin
craft pliers, smooth-jawed

Basic Frame Design

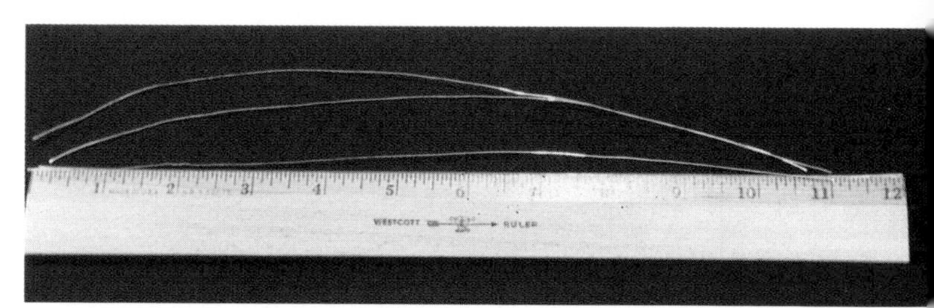

Cut three pieces of 24 gauge silver wire, each 11 inches long.

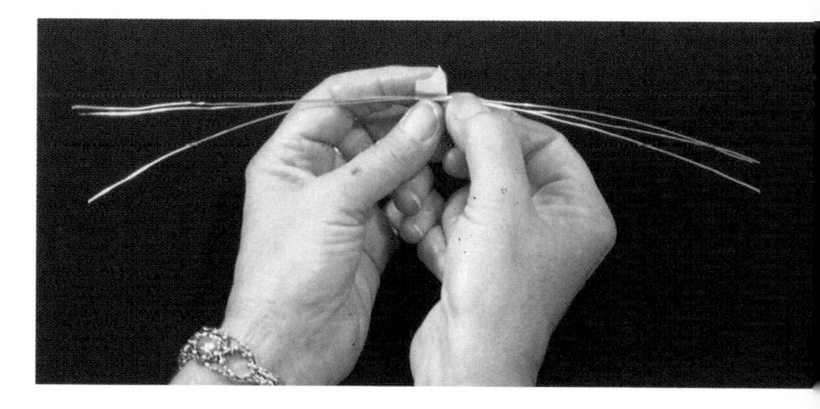

Hold the three strands of wire in one hand, laying side by side lengthwise, with the ends even. Measure 5 1/2 inches into the middle and tape the strands together at this point; this should be the center of the strands of wire.

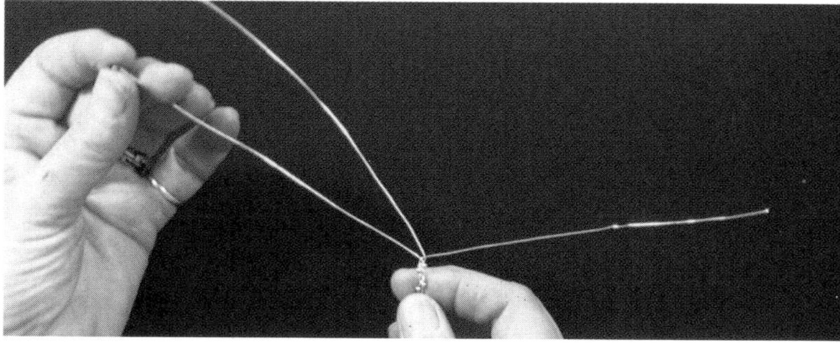

In this project, we will be using the Double-Sided frame bead pattern.

1 plain braid

Starting at the middle, bend the left outside wire over the center wire; then bend the right outside wire over the wire that is now in the center, to complete one plain braid.

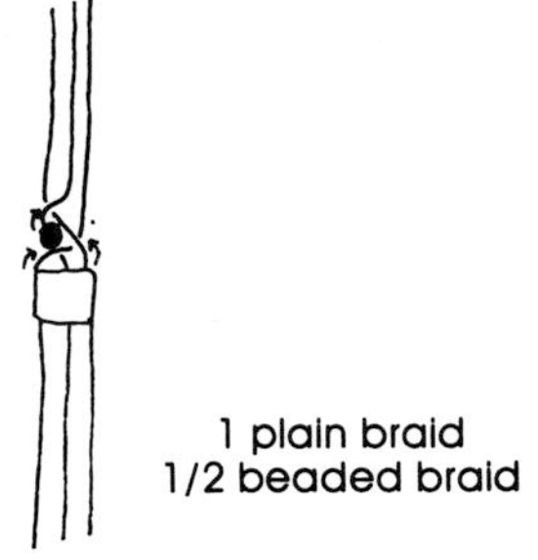

(*) Place one gold bead on the left outside wire. Then bend the left outside wire over the center wire.

Place one gold bead on the right outside wire. Then bend the right outside wire over the center wire.

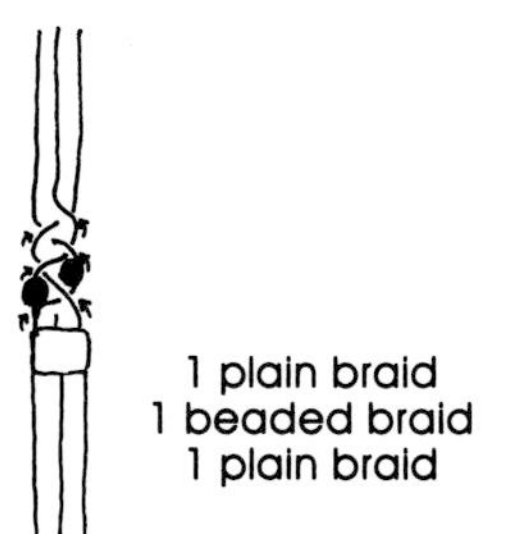

Without adding any beads, bend the left wire over the center wire. Then bend the right wire over the center.

Repeat from the (*) until you are 1/2 inch from the end of the three wires. When you are finished, there should be thirty gold beads on this half of the braided wire, between the tape at the center point and the end.

Your piece should look like the braid at the left, above. Notice that the gold beads are in diagonal pairs, with the beads on the right slightly higher than the beads on the left; this is normal. Flip the braid over so that the 'back' is facing up, and then rotate the piece so that the loose wires are facing upwards from your hands, ready to braid. Doing this will make the diagonal direction of the beads reverse, so that the left-hand beads are slightly higher, as in the braid illustrated at the right, above. From this position, remove the tape and all adhesive, and begin to work on the second half of your 11-inch wire braid. First, bend the right outside wire (without a bead) over the center wire, making half of a plain braid.

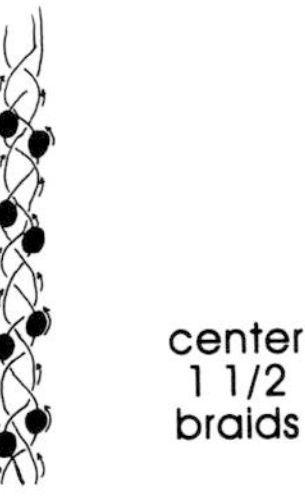

Since you started the first side of this project by making one plain braid at the tape before adding any beads, this new *half* of a plain braid will give you 1 1/2 plain braids at the center of your wires. This extra half-braid will reverse the diagonal slant of the beads you are about to add.

Now proceed adding beads in the same order as you did for the other side. Notice in this photograph how the diagonal slant of the bead pattern *reverses* in the middle (the switch can be seen right between my middle and ring fingers). After 15 sets of beads (30 beads in all) have been braided into the wire, finish that end of the wire by braiding it to the end without any beads. This unbeaded segment will be used to make the neckchain loop. Do *not* braid any further on the other side of the frame; it should end simply with its last bead, two plain braids, and three dangling wires.

Bending the Cross Shape

To start making the cross, bend the wire into a U-shape at the middle point, using your smooth-jawed needle-nose pliers to press the flat front surfaces of the braid together.

Once the wire is bent in half, the beads that ran on opposite diagonals earlier will all be in alignment. You will be able to see the diagonal bead pattern only when looking at the "U"-shape from the side. When the "U" is pushed tight together, the beads shaded in the illustration will be touching eachother, and the beads blackened in the illustration will be toching each other.

Looking at the cross from the front, you will only see ONE bead from each bead pair; the other will be on the reverse.

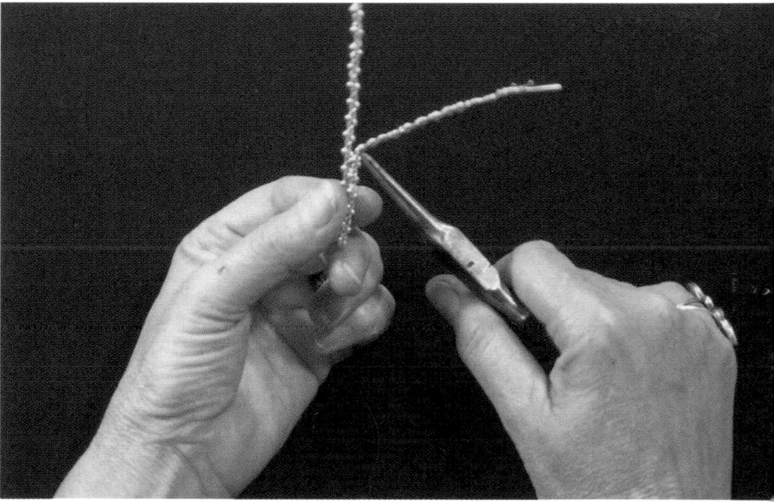

On one side of the U-shaped bend, count up four pairs of beads...

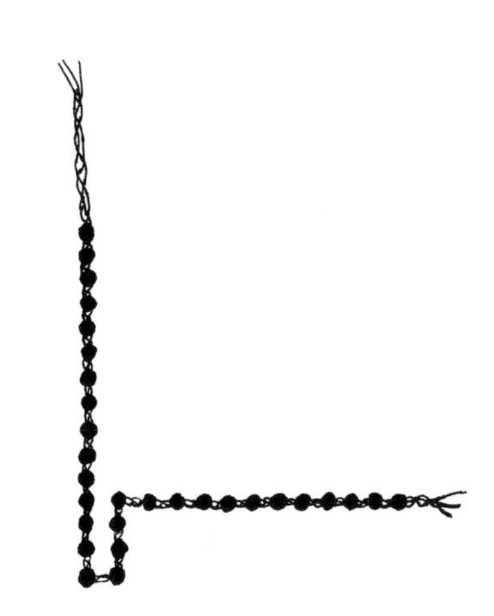

...and use the pliers to make a right-angle bend.

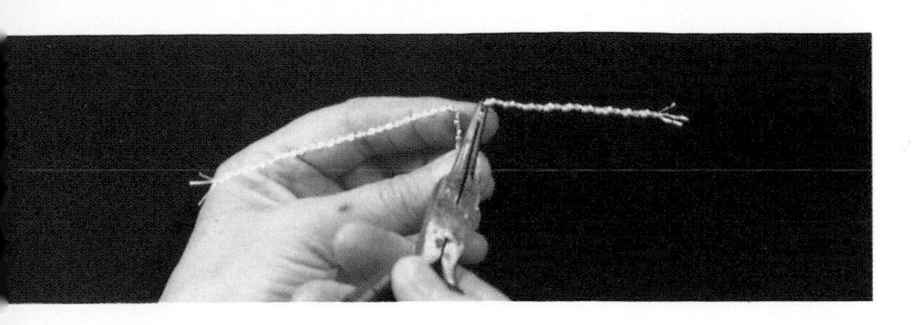

Do the same on the other side of the U-shaped bend.

These will form the arms of the cross.

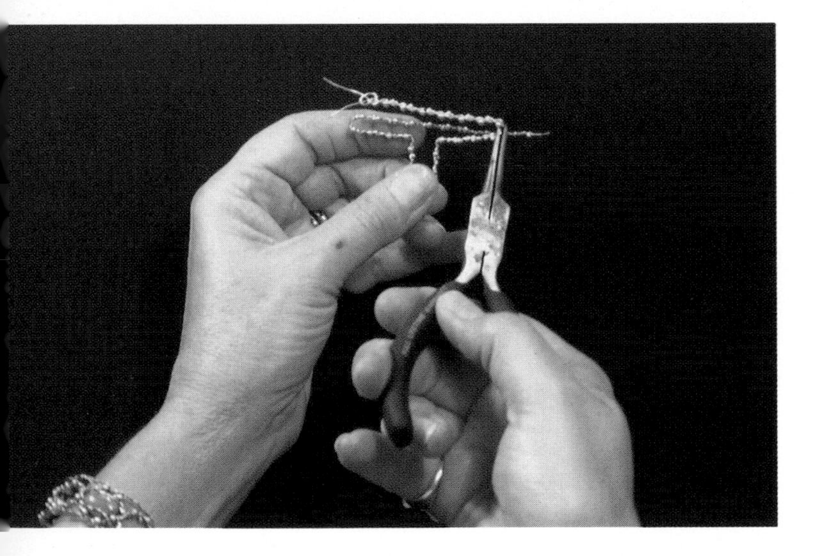

Count four beads down one arm, and bend it in an "elbow" back upon itself. Do the same on the other arm.

Your cross should now look like this.

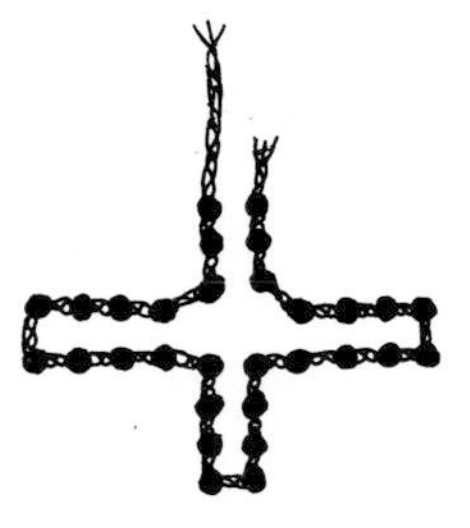

Count four beads from each of these last bends, and make a final set of bends.

This will complete the cross shape.

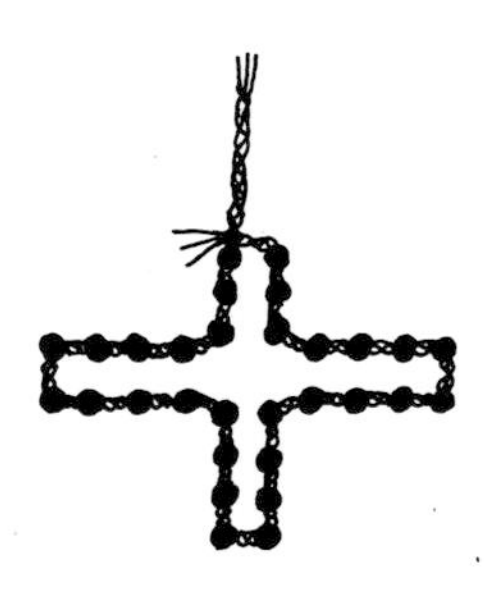

Use the needle-nose pliers to bend the final two braids and the dangling wires on the right towards the braided wire on the left.

To connect the frame, push the center unbraided wire through the opening at the top of the last bead on the left side. Hold the other two loose wires out of the way.

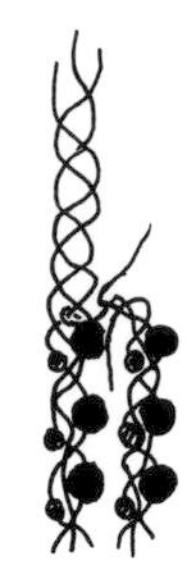

Bend this single wire back, and pass it through an adjacent opening. Cut it, and tuck the end out of sight. In this diagram (and in the next five) I have drawn both beads in each bead pair to show you the details of the connecting wire braids more effectively. The larger, black beads are the front ones that will be visible from the front of your cross; the shaded, smaller beads are the back beads,which you will not see when you look at the front of your actual piece.

At this point, the cross will be closed at the top. A braid will extend up to be used as the chain loop, and two spare wires will remain. Cut one of the spare wires short, and then tuck it away out of sight. Leave the other wire as it is for the time being.

Making the Chain Loop

Bend the braided end so that it makes a loop. The end of the loop should be touching the frame of the cross on the opposite side.

Pass the center wire of the chain loop braid down through the cross frame, between the last frame beads and the connecting braids. Bring it back up through another opening, and cut and tuck it out of sight.

Cut and tuck one of the remaining two wires. At this point there should be one dangling wire on each side of the chain loop—one from the end of the plain chain loop braid, and the earlier one from the beaded braid that made the body of the cross.

Use the needle-nosed plier to pinch the base of the chain loop closer together.

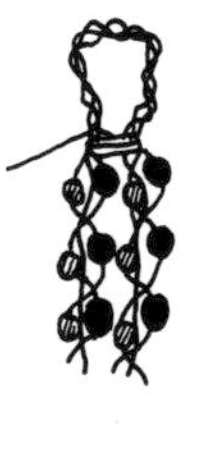

Then wrap the lone wire that was left from the chain loop braid around the base of the loop two or three times. Cut and tuck the end back into the braid.

Holding the cross in your fingers, use the pliers to gently twist the loop a half turn so that a chain will be able to pass through the loop and the cross will lay flat when it is worn.

The last loose wire can now be wrapped two or three times around the base of the chain loop, cut, and tucked away.

Here is a finished frame for the cross pendant. Notice that only one bead from each bead pair will be visible from the front.

As you become a more experienced jewelry-maker, you can add a number of variations to your frames; for instance, they can be make with gold beads on just one side of the braided wire, or on only the center wire.

Adding the Top and Bottom Beads

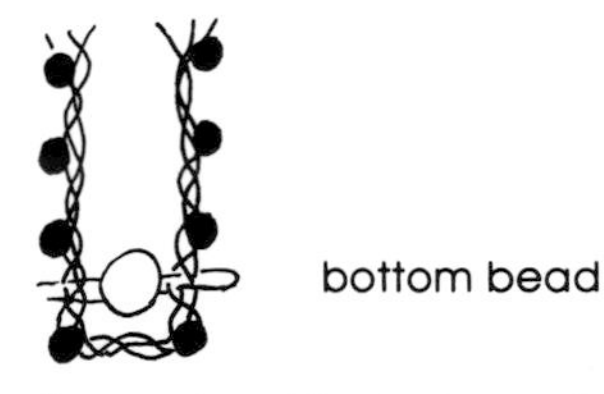

(*) Place one 4 mm (or 6 mm) stone bead in the base of the cross, aligning the holes with the sides of the frame. Cut a piece of 28 gauge wire, approximately 4 inches long; this will be your beading wire. Bend it in half and insert the ends through the braided frame as shown—each end in a separate opening—and through the bead.

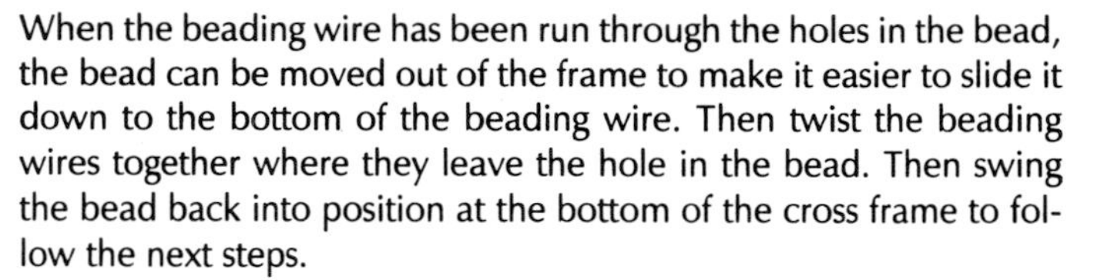

When the beading wire has been run through the holes in the bead, the bead can be moved out of the frame to make it easier to slide it down to the bottom of the beading wire. Then twist the beading wires together where they leave the hole in the bead. Then swing the bead back into position at the bottom of the cross frame to follow the next steps.

Then run the wires (twisted together) through a *single* opening in the braided frame. Holding both ends together, pull the beading wire tight.

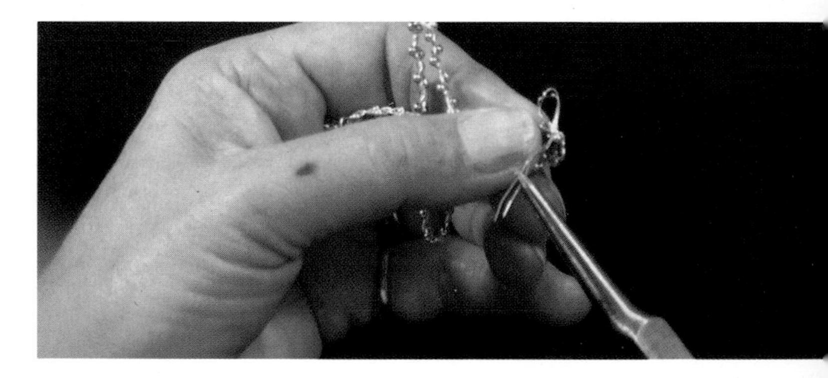

Still keeping them together, pass the ends back through an adjacent opening in the frame. If you have trouble getting the two twisted wires through this opening, use a small needle or pin and gently widen it until the wire fits.

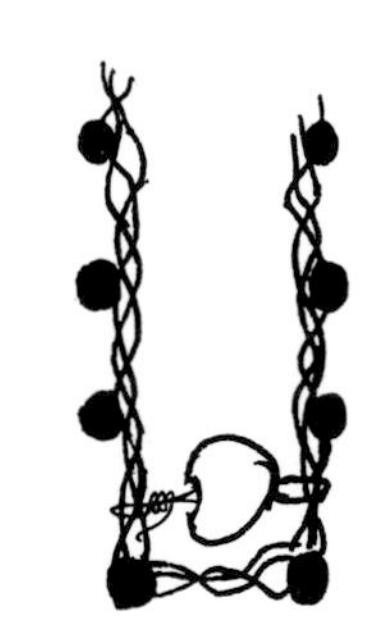

Keeping the beading wire snug, pull the loose ends back into the cross frame, up to the hole in the stone bead. There, wrap the loose ends around the twisted wire several times, to keep the bead in place. Cut the loose ends, and tuck them out of sight.

To wrap the frame around the bead, you will need a new piece of 22-gauge wire, crimped into a hook at one end.

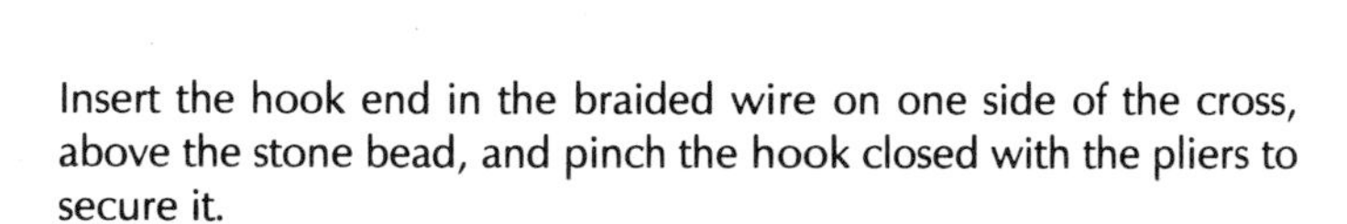

Insert the hook end in the braided wire on one side of the cross, above the stone bead, and pinch the hook closed with the pliers to secure it.

Using the pliers to grip the wrap wire, make two or three tight wraps.

While you are doing this, it is helpful to hold the cross in one hand with the stone bead securely between the thumb and fingers. After making the wraps, cut the wire just long enough to tuck it securely out of sight. Here you can see the bottom bead attached and wrapped to the cross frame. Follow these same steps (starting from the *) to attach the top bead.

Attaching the Side-Arm Beads

with a stone bead at center

The methods used for attaching stone beads to the side arms is not too different from the methods used for the top and bottom beads. First, cut a piece of beading wire 6 1/2 inches long. Bend it in half and insert each end of the beading wire through different openings at the end of one of the cross arms. Twist the full length of the beading wire.

Put a stone bead on the twisted wire and push it tight into the braid corner at the end of the arm.

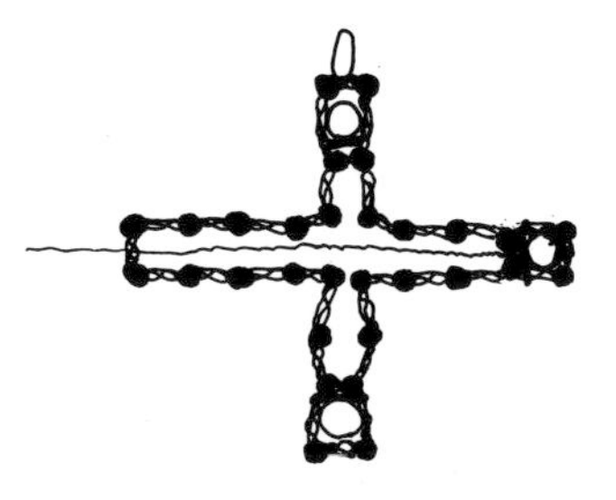

Wrap this bead just as you wrapped the bottom and top beads, with 22 gauge wire: make a crimp in the wire, insert the hook in the braid close to the bead, and pinch the crimp closed. Grip the wrap wire with the pliers, and make two or three wraps. Cut the wire just long enough to tuck out of sight.

You may choose to use another spherical stone bead in the center (for instructions on how to use a flat stone, see page --). To do this, string the stone bead on the beading wire, stopping at the center of the cross, and gently bend the frame around it. String on the last side-arm bead, but don't worry about its placement just yet.

Run the two ends of the twisted beading wire through a single opening at the end of the cross arm.

The run them back through an adjacent opening.

Wrap the end of the wires around the twisted segment just inside the cross frame, right before the last stone bead. Cut and tuck the ends out of sight.

The cross should look like this. Make sure that you haven't pulled the beading wire too tight, or the cross arms will bend up out of position.

Next, make the wrap around the second side-arm bead, just as you made the top, bottom, and first side wraps.

Here are the side-arm beads, in position and wrapped into place.

After that, cut and crimp wire to make the wraps on the sides, top, and bottom of the central stone bead.

You can use the pliers to pull the wraps securely.

Now, with a total of eight wraps, the cross should be finished.

Push the tip of the pliers through the sections of the frame between the beads to open them up. This will give the cross an airy, filigreed appearance. Be sure that you push the beading wire to follow the curve of the top or bottom frame braid, so that it is not visible. Once this is done, your cross is finished! It is not absolutely necessary to secure stone beads with epoxy glue, but I suggest doing it as a precaution anyway.

Adding the Side-Arm Beads

using a flat-backed stone at the center

Instead of using a spherical stone bead with a drilled hole at the center of your cross, you might want to use a flat-backed stone, either round-shaped or oval. The methods for this are slightly different. Instead of twisting the *entire* length of the beading wire running across the arms, you will need to leave a segment untwisted at the middle. This untwisted segment can then be spread open to make retaining wires for the stone, much like the ones made in this book's second project, the beaded stone frames.

To start, insert the beading wire through two openings in the right arm, and twist the wire for the length of the cross's arm, starting (in this example) at the right and stopping where the center space begins.

String on the first side-arm stone bead, sliding it all the way into the end of the arm. At the center of the cross, spread the beading wire open, as shown.

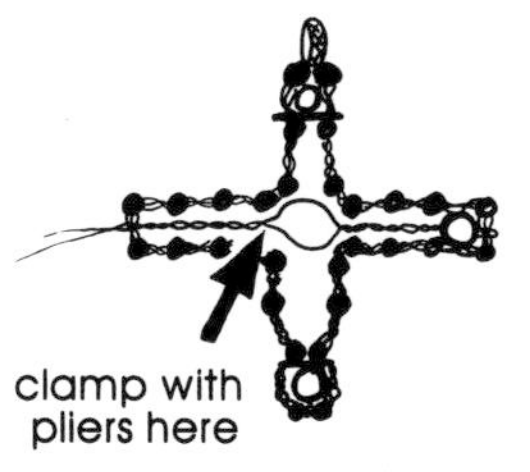

Then hold the beading wire with pliers at the end of the center area, after leaving an open, untwisted area of at least 1/4 inch, and resume twisting.

Twist all the way to the end of the beading wire, and add the second side-arm stone bead. Finally, thread the twisted beading wires through a single opening in the frame braid. Do not finish off the trailing ends of the beading wire yet.

Cut and crimp a hook into a piece of 22 gauge wire, and use the same wrapping techniques as you used earlier to secure the right side-arm stone bead in place. Next, lay the flat-backed stone in the center and press the braided wire gently around it to shape the frame. Once you have satisfactorily done this, set the flat-backed stone aside; the shaped frame will show you where to position the wrap wires for the center of the cross.

Still using 22 gauge wire, add wraps at the top, bottom, and both sides of the center stone position.

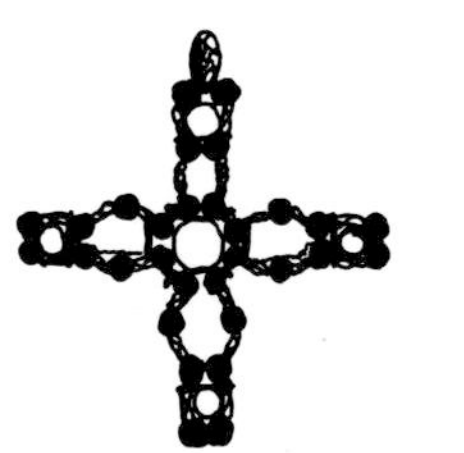

Push the tip of the pliers through the arm space bewteen the right-hand and center stones and open the frame. Be careful to flatten the beading wire against one side of the cross frame so that it doesn't show. Since you still have the loose ends of the beading wire dangling, thread them back through an opening in the frame; cut and tuck, as usual, to finish off that wire. Then wrap the left side-arm stone bead with 22 gauge wire and open that cross arm with the pliers.

Now you can put the center stone back in place.

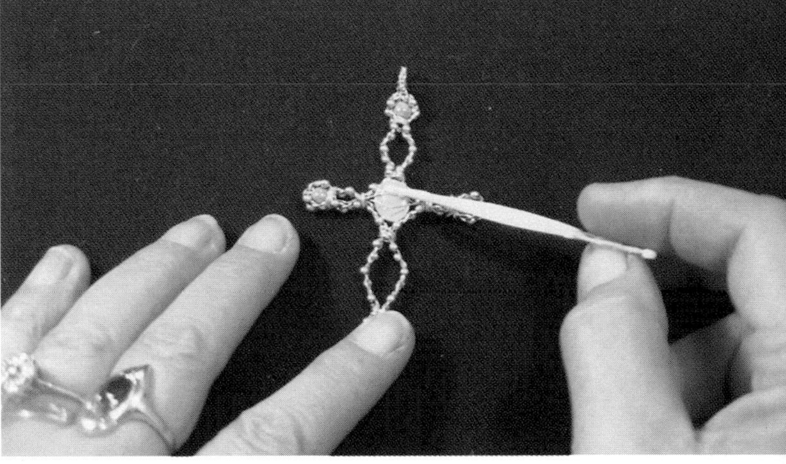

To secure the flat-backed stone to the retaining wires, turn the cross back-side up and mix some two-ton, five-minute epoxy. Using a toothpick or a needle, put the glue on the back of the stone and the beading wire to hold them together.

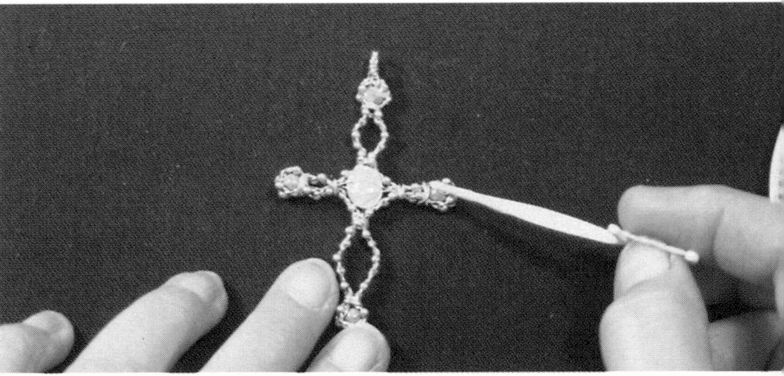

For added security on the stone beads at the ends of the cross arms, put a small amount of the glue on their wraps. Your cross is finished!

Project #5
MONKEY
Necklace or Pin

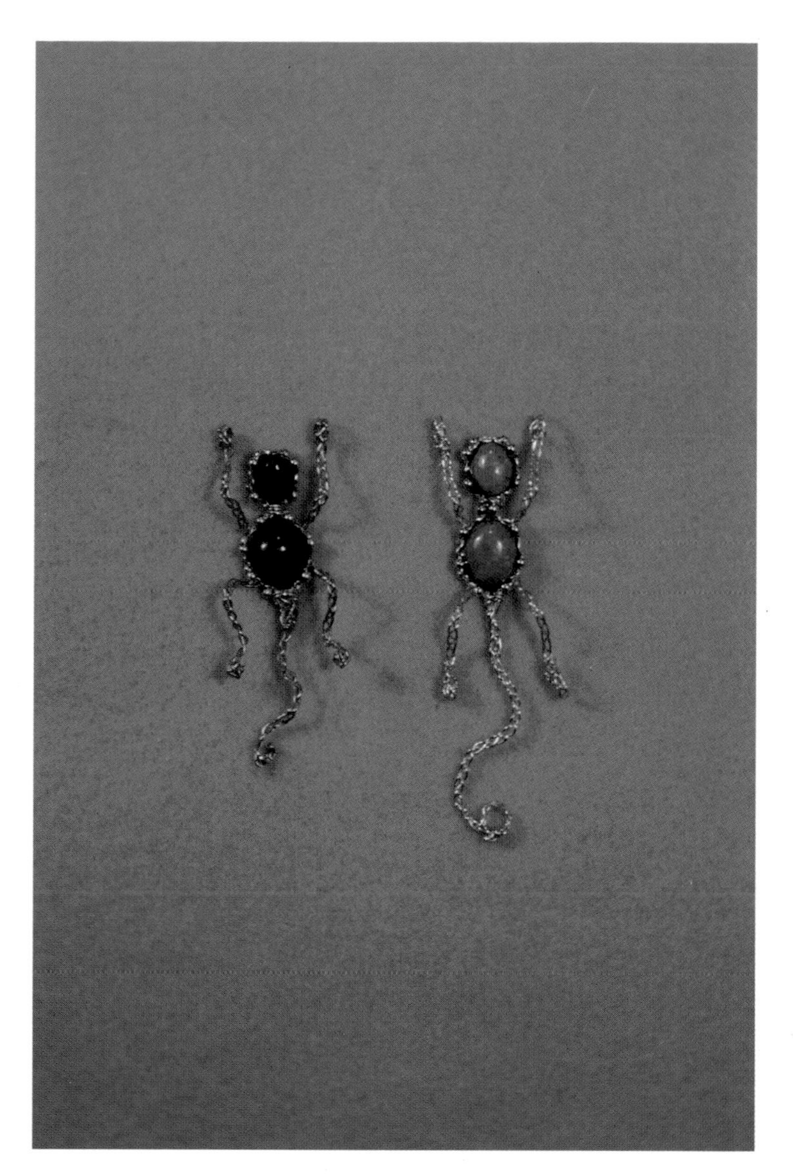

MATERIALS

24 gauge gold or sterling silver wire
22 gauge wrapping wire in contrasting color
2 mm sterling silver or gold frame beads
28 gauge beading wire
2 flat-backed stones: one 8 mm,
    one 12 mm

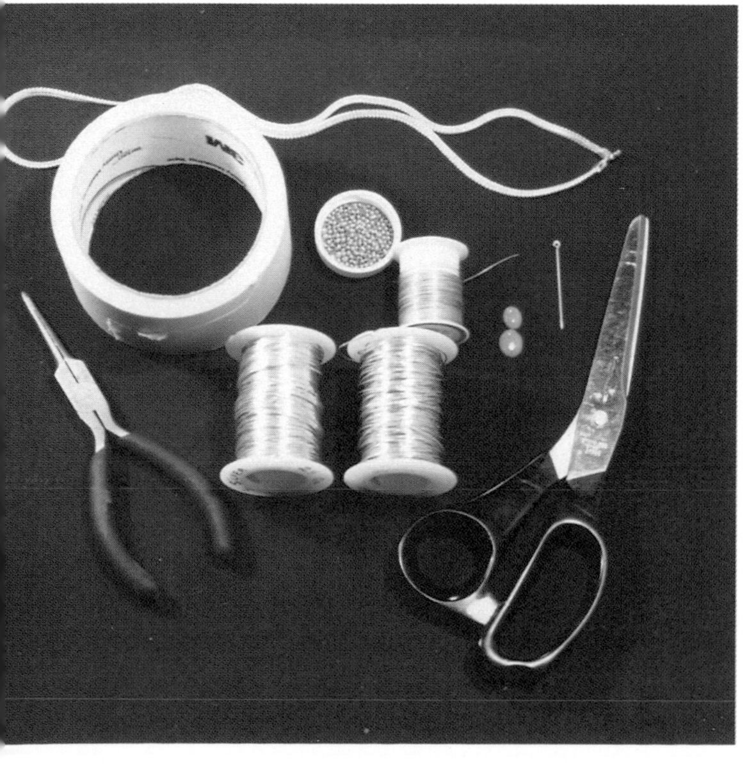

TOOLS

masking tape
smooth-jawed needle-nose pliers
scissors (to cut wire)
needle or pin

Making the Frame

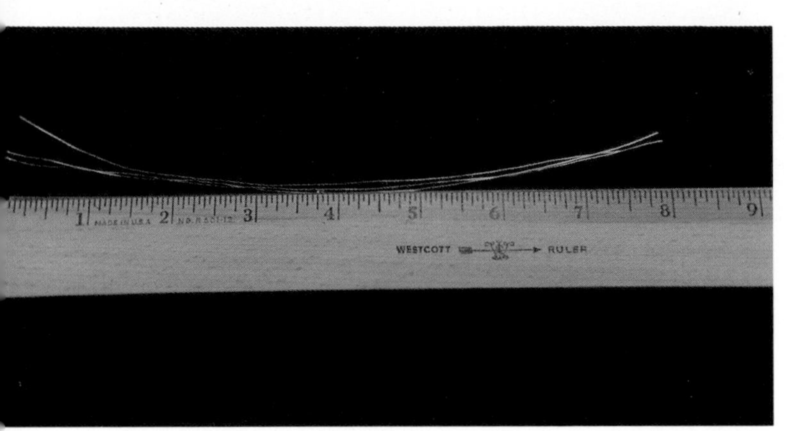

Measure and cut three pieces of 24 gauge wire, each 8 inches long.

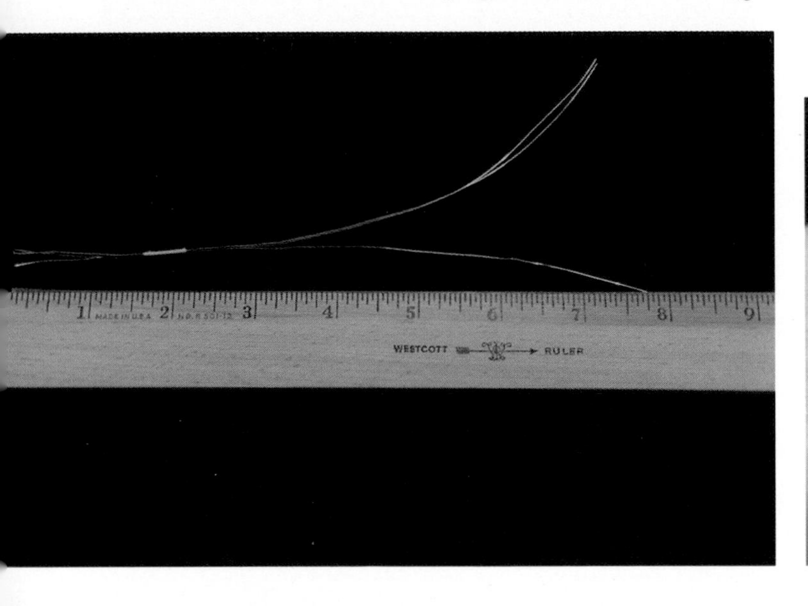

Holding the three pieces of wire together, measure 1 1/2 inches from one end and place a piece of 1/4 inch wide masking tape at that point, as I have done here.

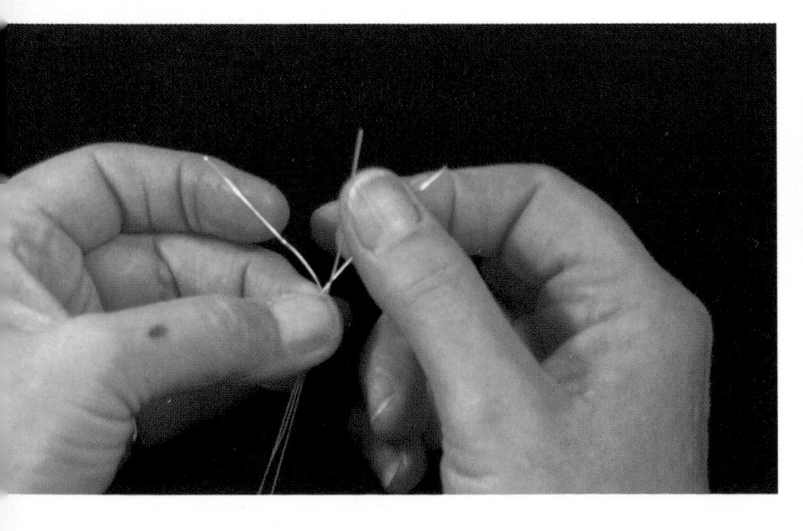

Start braiding the 1 1/2 inch segment, beginning at the masking tape. (*) Make one complete plan braid by crossing the left wire over the center wire, and then the right wire over the center wire.

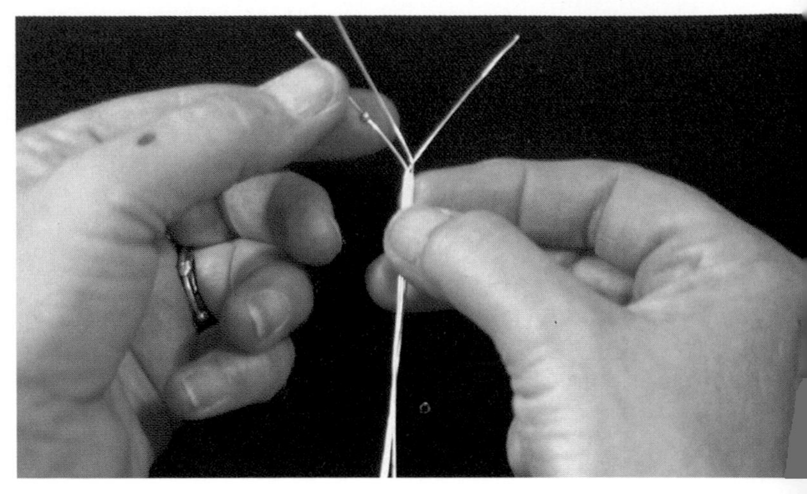

This project will be made using the Double-Sided frame bead pattern. To start, place one framing bead on the left wire, and then bend the left wire over the middle wire.

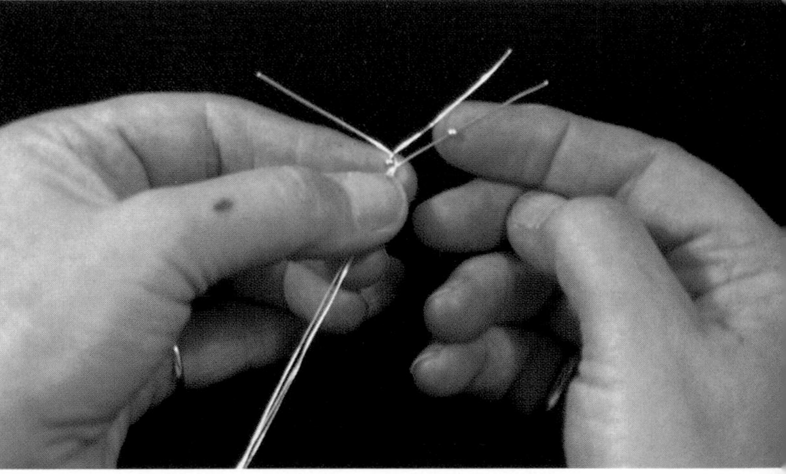

Put a framing bead on the right wire, and then bend the right wire over the middle wire. You will need to make one plain braid between each bead pair.

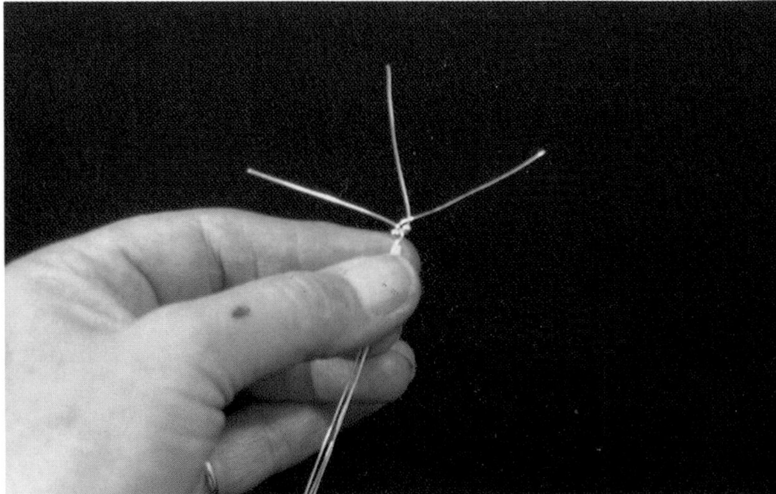

If the braid seems too loose, use the pliers to squeeze the braids tighter.

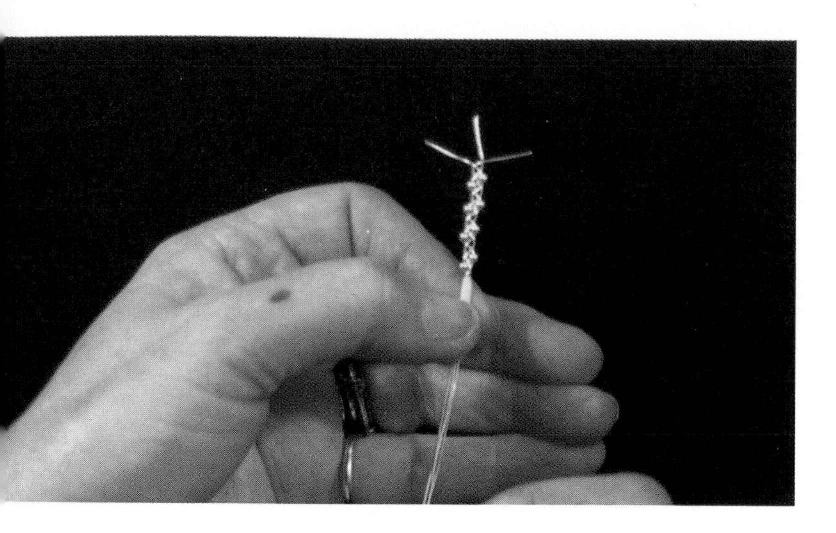

Repeat from the * until approximately 1/4 inch of unbraided wire remains.

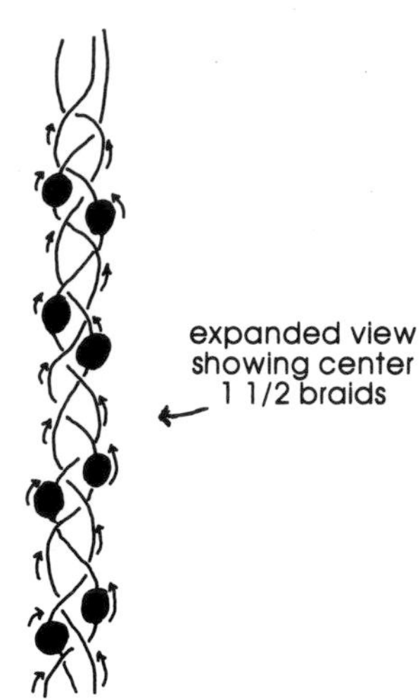

To resume braiding in the other direction, cross the right wire over the center wire to make half of a plain braid. This will give you 1 1/2 plain braids between your first beaded segment and the one you are about to begin. Now go back to the instructions beginning at the * and work up from the 1 1/2 plain braids, incorporating beads on alternate sides.

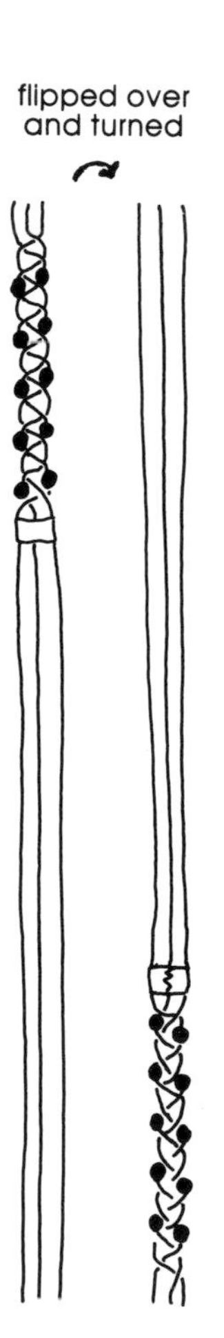

Remove the masking tape and all the adhesive from the wire; flip the piece over to the back side, and rotate it upside-down so that the loose wires are pointing up from your hands.

Continue until there is an equal number of framing beads on both ends, leaving approximately 4 to 5 inches of unbraided wires on the second end. Notice that the diagonal slant of the bead pairs will reverse, just as they did in the cross pendant (Project #4).

To begin shaping the monkey, find the center of the braided portion of the wire—the 1 1/2 plain braids where my index finger is pointing.

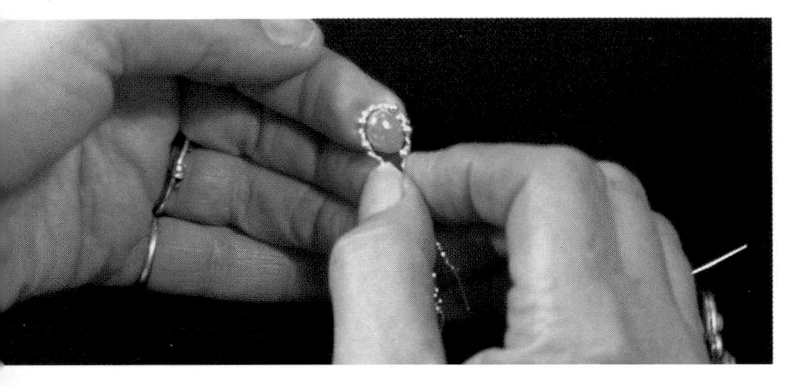

Place the 8 mm flat-backed stone next to the wire and bend the braided wire around the stone. This will make the head of the monkey.

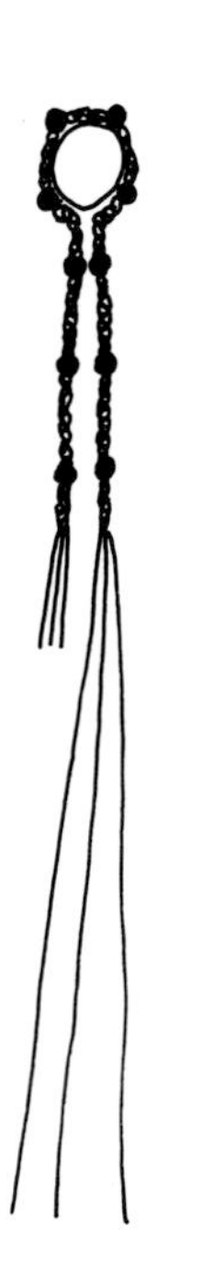

Be sure that you have the stone centered longways and that the beads make a symmetrical pattern on either side. Gently press the braided frame around the edges of the stone, and squeeze them together when they meet at the bottom (6 o'clock) of the stone.

Remove the stone, and wrap the bottom of the braided wire loop with 22 gauge wrapping wire in a contrasting color—that is, use a gold wrap if your frame is silver, a silver wrap if your frame is gold. To start wrapping, make a crimp in the end of a segment of wrapping wire. Insert the crimp into an opening as close to the bottom of the stone position as possible, and pinch the crimp closed around the wire.

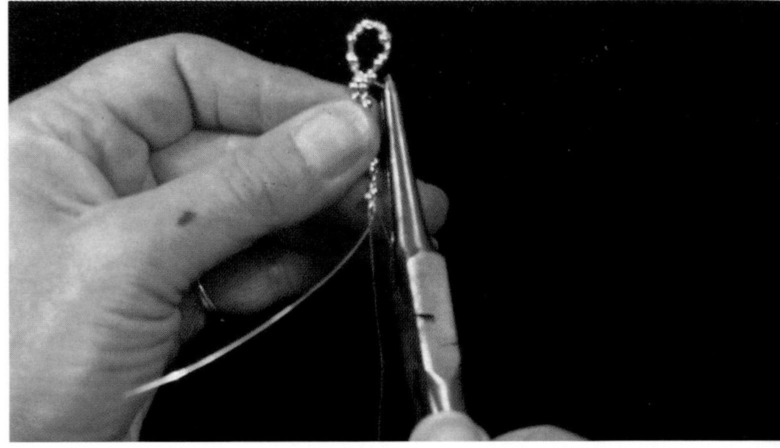

Wrap the wire in two or three tight turns around the braided wire ends, and then cut the wrapping wire just long enough to tuck the end out of sight.

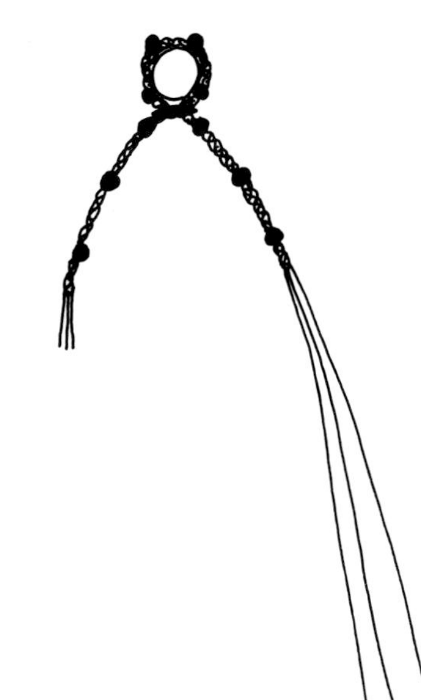

Putting the 8 mm stone back into the frame to be sure that it still fits may be difficult; if so, I recommend using the pliers to gently press the stone into the frame. Cover the top of the stone with masking tape to protect it before you do this. Fit it into the frame so that the back is flush with the base of the braided wire frame, and then remove it again and set it aside. You may have to use the point of the pliers to push it out from the back. If the stone does NOT fit back into the wrapped frame, you will have to undo the wrap, refit the stone, and wrap it again for a better fit.

Place the 12 mm flat-backed stone—the monkey's body—in the open area below the head, where you just finished the wrap. The braided segments of wire hanging down on either side of the body should be of equal length (though one side will have an extra 4 or 5 inches of unbraided wire). Use the pliers to bend these beaded braids into a frame around the 12 mm stone. Be sure that the framing beads are symmetrical from side to side. Gently press the braided wire from each side together at the base. Remove the stone so that you can finish the frame, but do not wrap it yet! First, the monkey's tail must be braided from the six dangling wires (three short ones on one side, and three long ones on the other).

Making the Tail

Before you begin the tail braid, hold the sides of the frame together once more. Make sure that no framing beads will fall below the wrap at the base of the body; there should be no beads in the tail. If there are, carefully unbraid the wire and remove them.

Now you are ready to make the braid out of the six dangling wires.

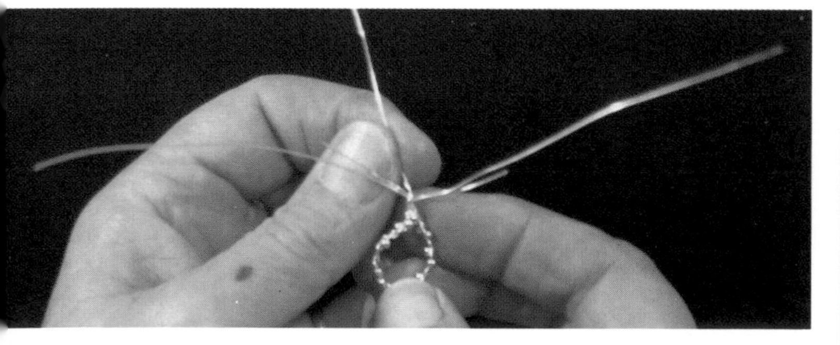

First, press the unbraided wires from each side together, matching the two right outside wires (one short with one long), the two left outside wires (one short and one long), and the two middle wires (one short and one long). In this photograph, you can see the three sets this makes.

Braid the left-side pair over the middle pair; then braid the right-side pair over the middle pair, to complete one plain braid. It is important that this braiding be tight. If it isn't, use the pliers to gently squeeze the braids tighter.

To make the tail taper, growing thinner towards the end, you will need to gradually reduce the number of braiding wires. To do this, hold the braid between your thumb and fingers. Grasp the short middle wire with the pliers, bend it, and push it up through an opening in the braid. If it is too long to tuck away, you can cut it to a manageable length.

Next, braid the pair of wires from the left side over the single remaining middle wire. Repeat the short wire tucking procedure with this pair. Finally, braid the pair of wires from the right side over the center wire, and cut and tuck the last of the short wires.

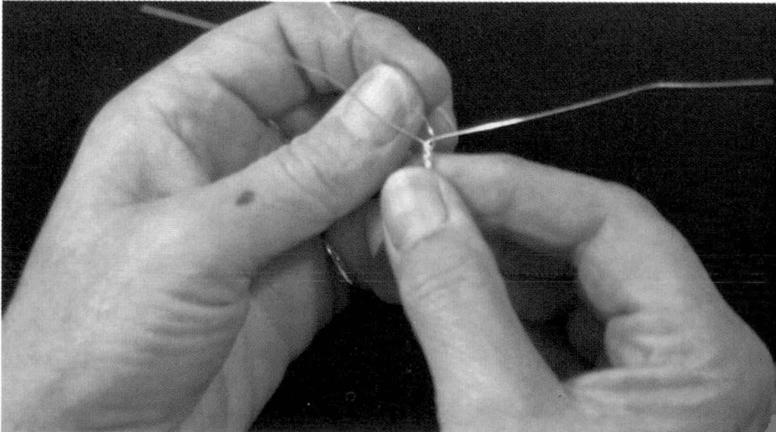

You should now be left with three single wires. Continue braiding until the tail is as long as you'd like it to be.

If you want the monkey to hang by its tail from your necklace, you will need to make a good-sized loop at the end of the tail. First, cut and tuck the two outside wires back into the braid, leaving the center wire loose.

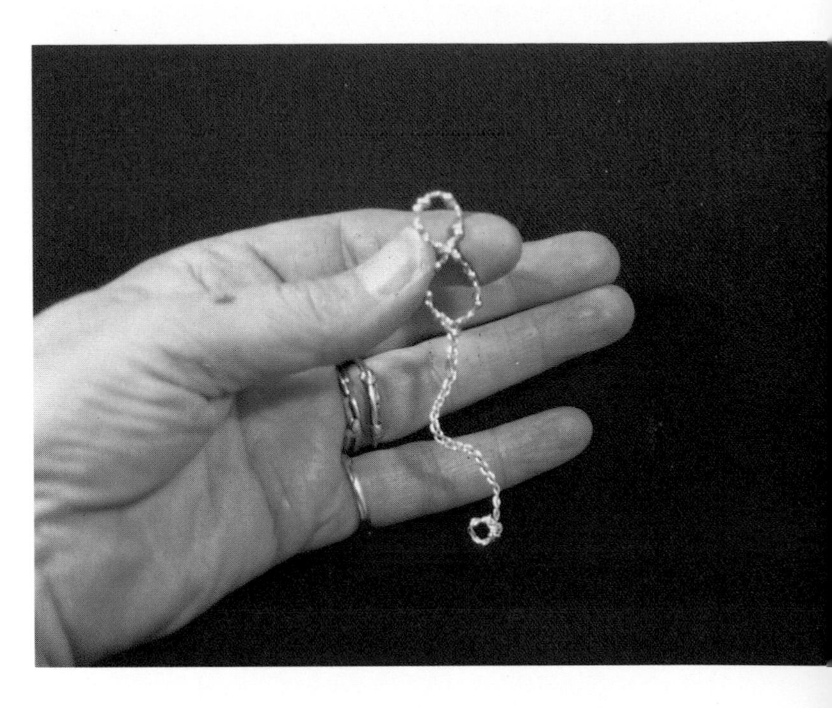

Here is a completed body frame with a looped tail. Even if you don't want the monkey to hang by its tail, you will still need to make a loop; I have found that when I just cut and tuck the end of the tail, the braid tends to spread out at the tip, actually looking like a tassel. If your loop is going to be purely decorative, rather than for a chain to pass though, you can use a very small nail to make a tiny loop.

Then bend the braided wire over a nail or something round. Be sure that the nail is large enough for a neckchain to pass through easily. Wrap the end of the braided loop around the nail until it touches the braided wire on the other side. Push the center wire through a braid opening there, to make a full circle.

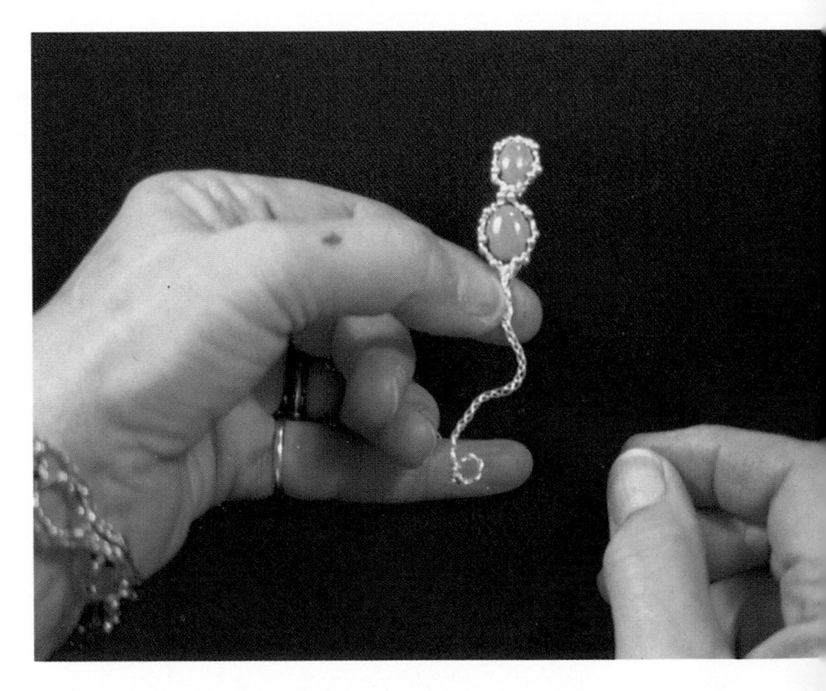

Place 12 mm stones back in the body frame and pinch the frame back around it (here I replaced the 8 mm stone in the head frame too, to give you an idea of how the finished piece will look). The spot where the two sides of the body frame meet at the base of the 12 mm stone is where you will make the wrap with 22 gauge wire (in a contrasting color, as explained before). Decide where the wrap must start, and then close the body frame loop just as you did the head frame loop: cut the 22 gauge wire, crimp, insert, pinch, wrap, cut, and tuck. There should be no framing beads below the wrap. Use the pliers to twist the tail a half-turn, so that the braid pattern is facing the front.

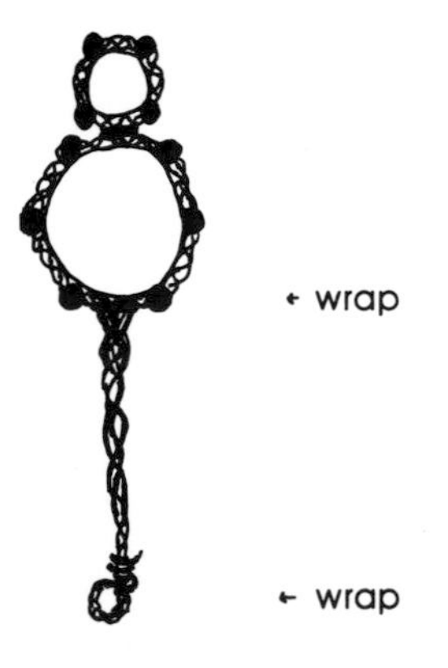

Then wrap the loose wire around the tail two or three times. Tuck the wire out of sight at the end of the wrap. Now remove the nail.

Making the Arms & Legs

To make the limbs of the monkey, you will need to cut six pieces of 24 gauge wire, each 4 inches long. Make two bundles of three wires each, one for the legs and the other for the arms.

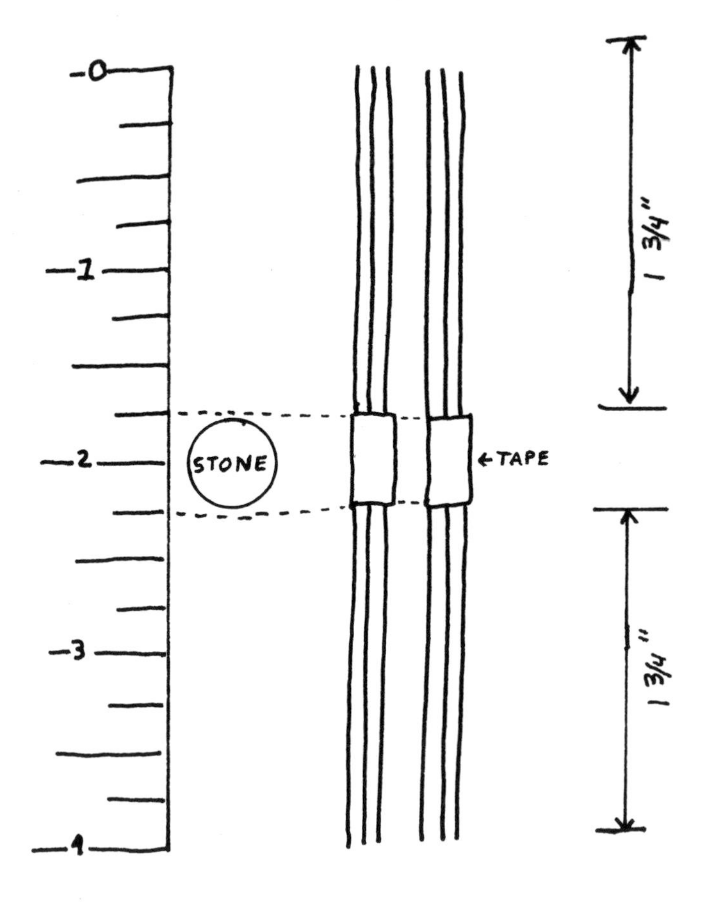

These bundles will be braided, but a short segment (the width of the flat-backed stone used for the body) must be left unbraided at the exact center of the bundle. To do this, measure across the stone; this one is 1/2 inch. Find the center of the bundle of wires, and measure out HALF of the stone width (1/4 inch) on either side of the center point. Finally, tape over this measured-off segment, so that it can remain unbraided as you braid the wires to either side of the taped center. You will need to do this to BOTH of the 6 inch bundles.

Braid the arm bundle, starting at the tape and braiding almost all the way to one end. Do the same to the leg bundle.

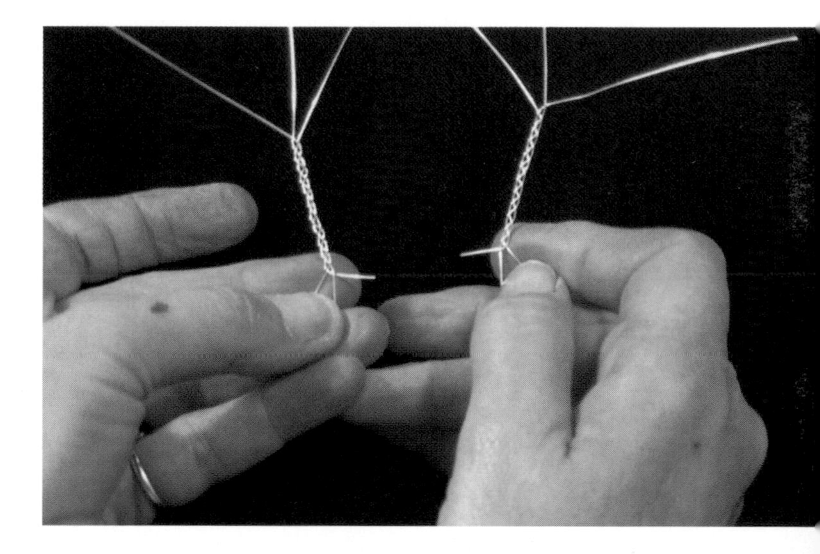

Then remove the tape and all the adhesive residue.

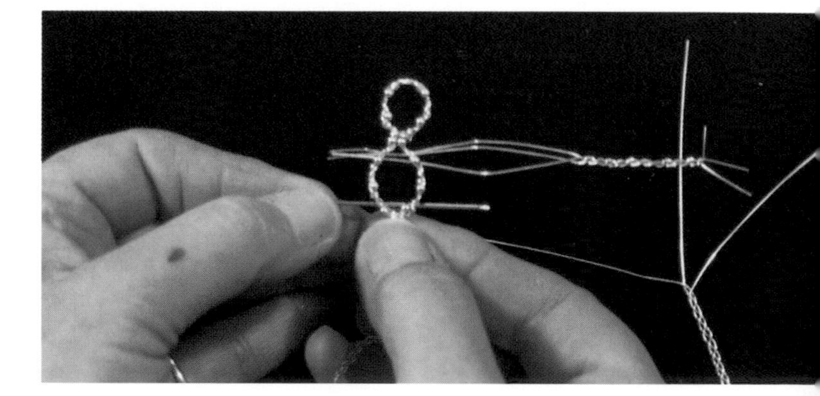

To make the arms, you will need to stretch the unbraided segment across the monkey's body frame. First, thread each unbraided wire from the arm bundle through a different opening in the body frame (close below the neck wrap) and out an opening in the opposite side. Do *not* insert all three wires in or out of the same opening in the frame; if you do, the arms will be able to be pulled out. You can use a pin or needle to widen the openings if you need to, as I am doing on the lower part of the body frame here.

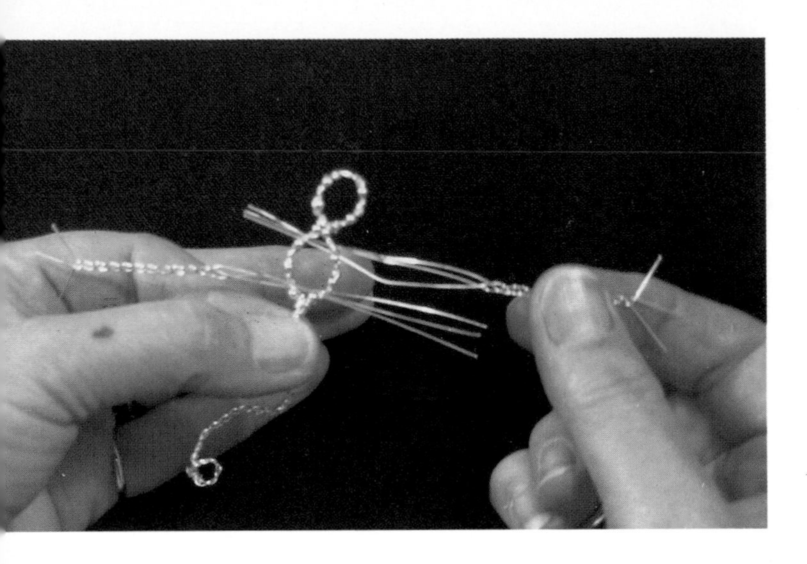

Do the same thing lower down on the body frame to make the legs.

Braid the portions of the wire that are protruding from the frame to make the second arm and the second leg. The segments that stretch through the body-area itself will remain unbraided, to serve as the backing for the flat-backed stone.

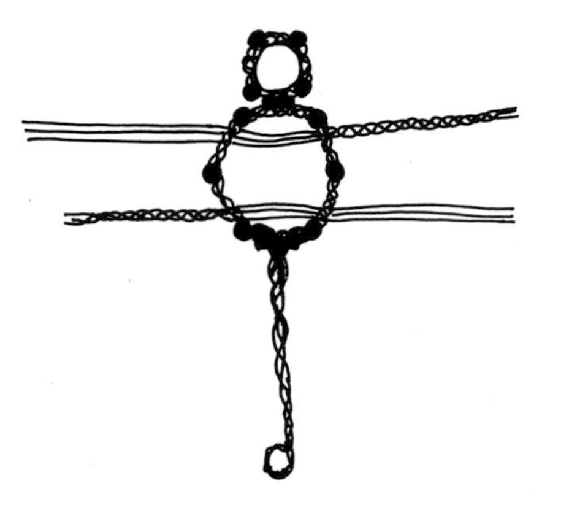

Pull the unbraided ends of the leg and arm wires all the way through the openings, so that the beginning of the braiding is snug up against the outside edges of the frame.

Use the pliers to spread out the backing wires, to give support to the flat-backed stone that will be used for the body.

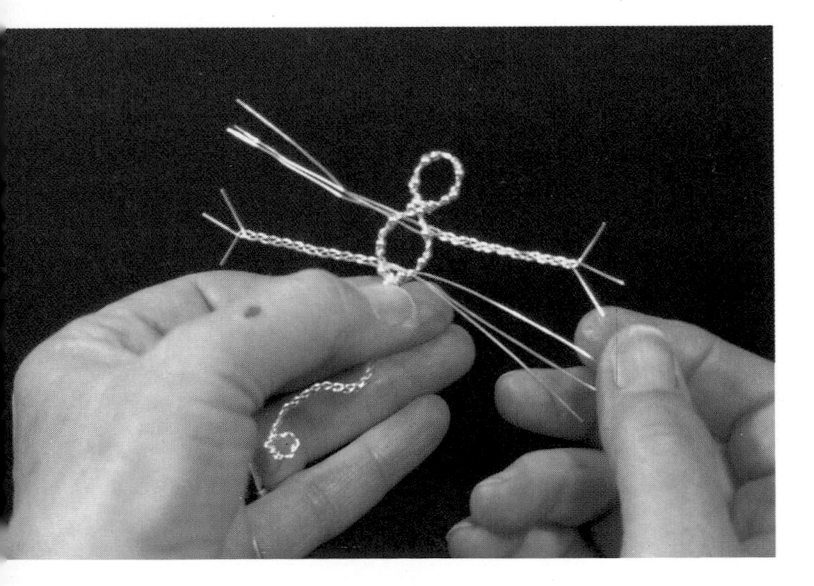

Your monkey should look like this.

To make the backing wires for the head frame stone, cut a piece of 28 gauge beading wire 4 to 6 inches long, and attach it to the back of the head frame with a crimp. Run it through openings in the frame, in and out in a criss-cross fashion; no specific pattern is necessary. Just be sure to provide a solid support for the flat-backed stone that will be used as the head.

Here are both the stones in their proper places.

To make the hands and feet of the monkey, you will use the same steps as those used to make the tail loop. First, cut and tuck the outside wires of each braid, leaving the center wire loose. Then, using the pliers or a nail, roll the braided wire at the end of the arms and legs so that they look like hands and feet.

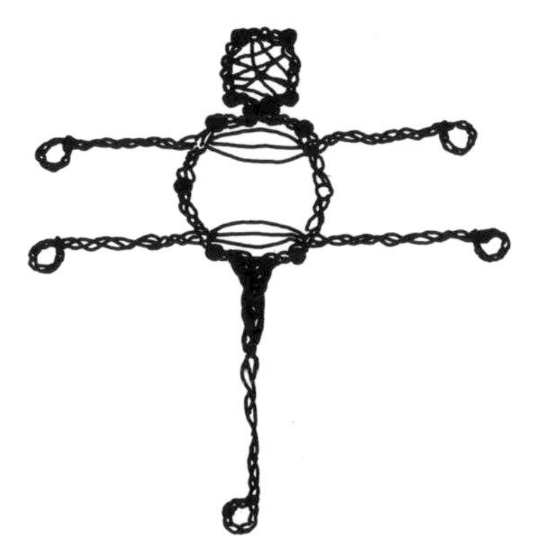

Thread the loose center wire of each braid through an opening in that braid, and wrap it around several times to secure the small hand or foot loop. Cut and tuck any loose ends. Now the monkey can be worn on a chain hanging either by his tail or by his hands.

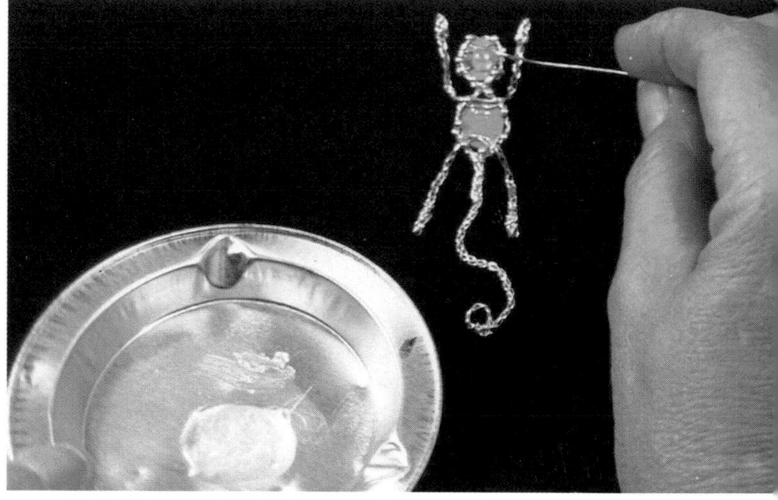

Finally, turn the monkey over (with the stones in their frames) and glue them in place with two-ton epoxy. Let the monkey set for 24 to 48 hours before touching it. I have found that dabbing a small amount of this glue on the back side of the tail, where the short wires were clipped and tucked to taper it, helps to hold the wires in place.

After the piece is entirely dry, put your finger on the back of the wire halfway down each leg to bend in the monkey's "knees." Do the same thing with the arms to make elbows.

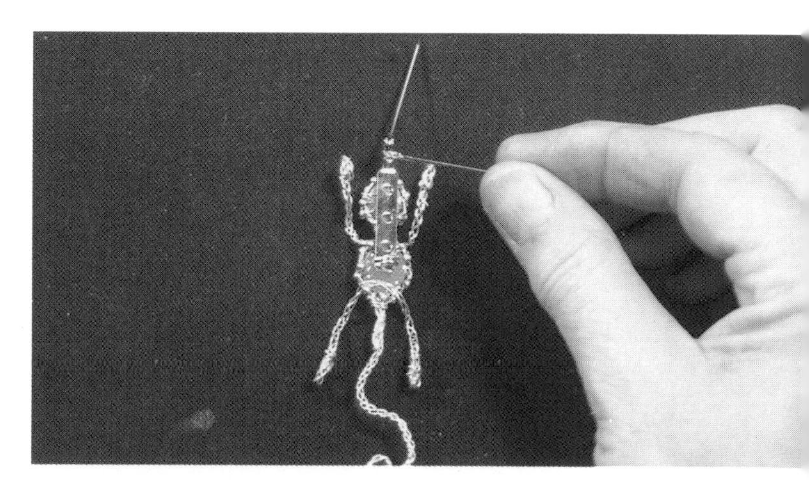

If you are going to use the monkey as a pin, buy a pin-back the length of the monkey's head and body. Glue it with the hinge end at the head and the latch end at the base of the body—and your monkey is ready to go!

Project #6

Women's WATCH BAND

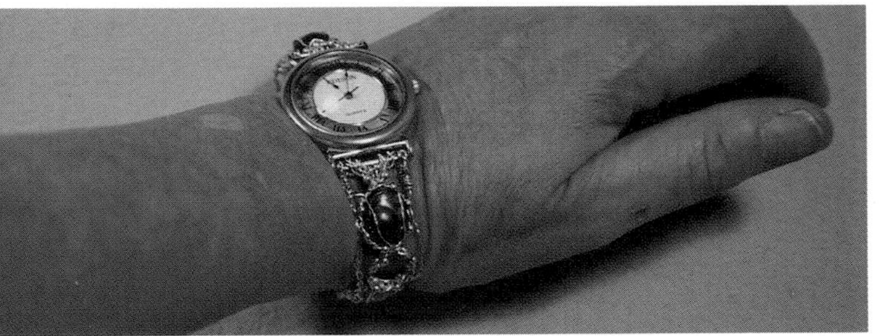

MATERIALS

24 gauge silver wire
24 gauge gold wire
2 mm gold beads (frame beads)
a watch-face
four 10 mm x 12 mm gem stones

TOOLS

ruler
masking tape
smooth-jawed needle-nose pliers
wire-cutters or scissors
pin or needle

The watchband is made in two halves, one for each side of the watch face. Each of these halves, in turn, consists of an silver inner band of open loops and stone frames (alternating), surrounded by an outer border of gold wire.

When you are measuring for a watch band or a bracelet, measure around the wrist; this is the length that the finished item will need to be. For the watchband, divide the number by 2 for the finished length on each side of the watch.

The average wrist measures 6 1/2 to 7 inches around, so each side of the finished watchband should be 3 1/4 to 3 1/2 inches long. For the band pattern given in this book, each side measures 3 1/4 inches when finished: a total of 6 1/2 inches. The measurements provided in the chart below reflect the amount of wire needed to braid one side of a watchband, as well as the amount taken up by the stone frames and the open loops in the band. The "unbraided" column gives the length of the three straight wires to be cut from your roll to make one half of the watchband. The length "after braiding" shows how long the three wires would be if they were to be braided in a straight line. For the watchband, the total (8 inches) should be divided by 2, which equals 4 inches. If you subtract 3 1/4 inches (the finished length) from 4 inches you will get the approximate width of the watchband, which is 3/4 inches.

The "Element" column lists the different parts that make up a finished watchband. If you read across from each element, you can see how much braided and unbraided wire is taken up by the different elements, and how much each of them contribute to the finished length of the band.

ELEMENT	WIRE (before braiding)	LENGTH (after braiding)	FINISHED LENGTH
Hook or Loop	1 5/8"	1 1/2"	5/8"
Beaded Open Loop	1 3/4"	1 1/4"	5/8"
Stone Frame	1 3/4"	1 1/4"	5/8"
Open Loop	1 3/4"	1 3/4"	5/8"
Stone Frame		1 1/4"	5/8"
Slide Pin Bar	7/8"	1/2"	1/8" top side
Wrap and Retainers	2 1/2"	0	3/8" under side
TOTAL	13"	8"	3 1/4"

To reduce the pattern, omit one braid above and one braid below the bead in each of the open beaded loops (see diagram).

To enlarge the pattern, add one braid in these places instead. This adds 1/4 inch to each half of the pattern's finished length, making it 3 1/2 inches on each side. You will need to add an extra 3/4 inch when you cut each of the three 13-inch lengths of unbraided wire to make the larger size watchband.

The open loops can come in handy if you need to make minor changes in the length of your band after you're done the project. If you find that the finished band is just a little too large, it can be adjusted by spreading the open loops a little wider. If the band is a little too tight, the open loops can be squeezed together just a little to give more length.

As you look at the diagrams in this section, keep in mind that I have drawn the braids *loose* to make it easier to follow; be sure to make your own braids tight and snug.

Making the Inner Loop Band

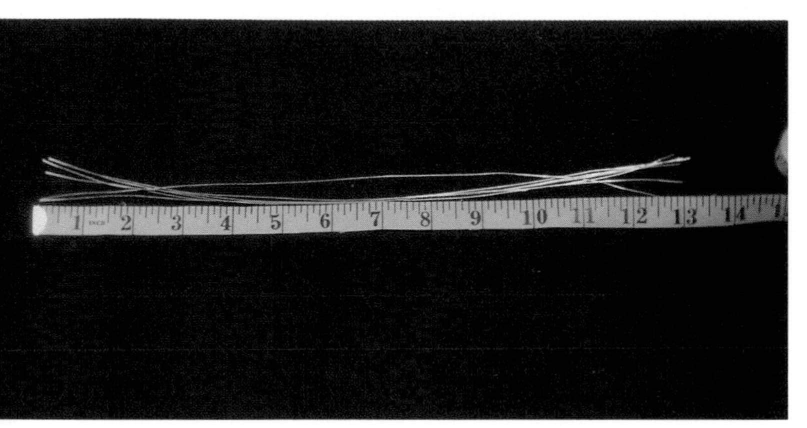

Cut six 24 gauge silver wires, three for each half of the watchband. These wires should be 13 inches long for a small to medium size wrist, 14 inches long for a larger wrist. Here I will use the smaller measurements. These wires will be used to make the *inside* section of the watchband, consisting of alternating open loops and stone frames.

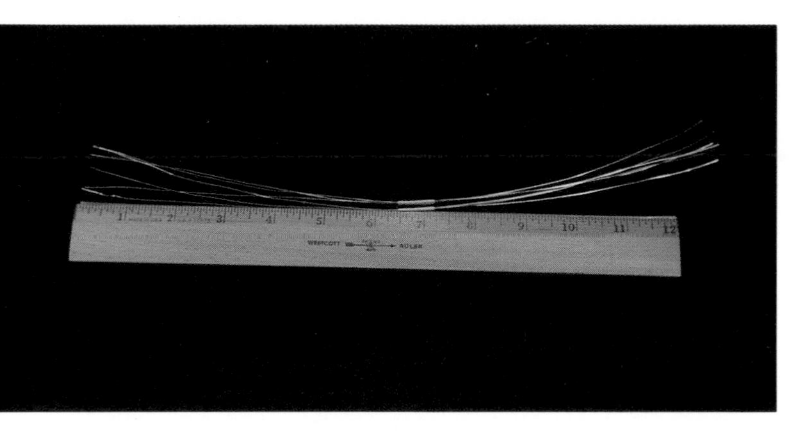

*Lay the wires side by side, in two bundles of three wires apiece, with the ends even. Measure in to the center of each bundle, and tape the wires together at that point.

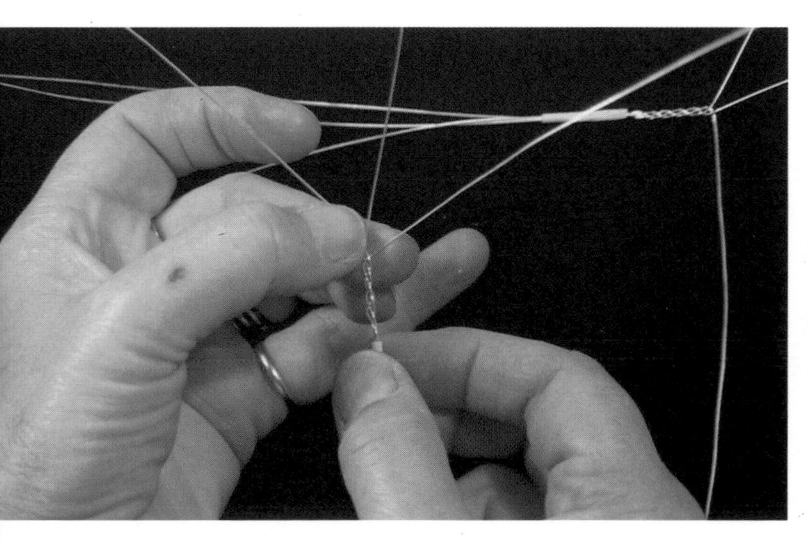

Start braiding at the center of the bundle, at the edge of the tape. Make seven plain braids.

Then remove the tape, and work out from the center to make 7 1/2 braids on the other side, for a total of 14 1/2 braids.

Do the same thing to the second bundle, so that it has 14 1/2 braids too. Remember, everything you do to one bundle has to be done to the other, since (except for the clasp) the two sides of the watchband will be identical! I recommend alternating between the two halves step-by-step, to make it easier to keep them identical.

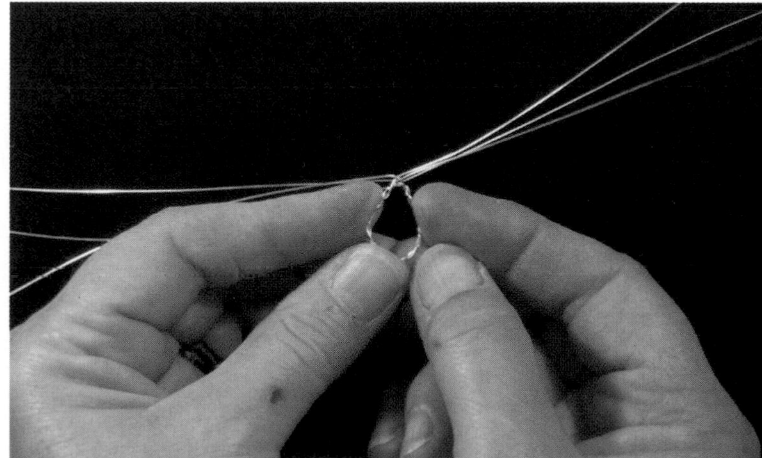

Bend the braided portion into a loop...

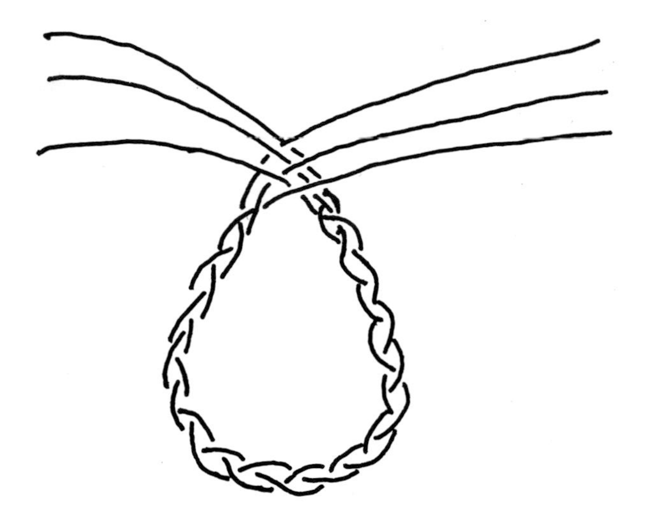

...so that the unbraided wires can be woven into a 'criss-cross'.

Here I am holding the loop (hidden) in my fingers so you can see a top view of the criss-cross at center, flanked by the left and right sets of wires—each with a tight plain braid, a beaded braid, and a plain braid.

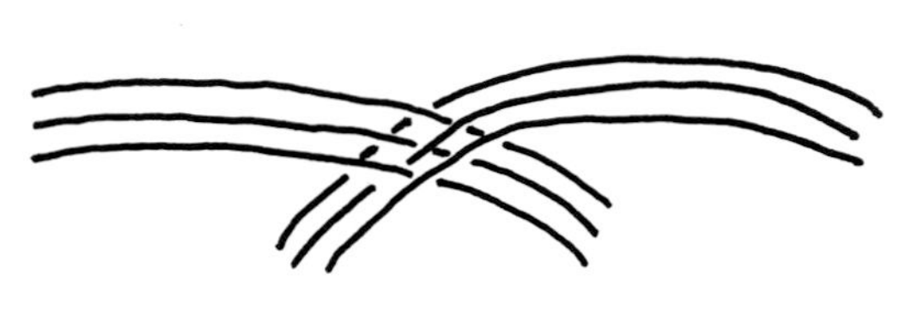

In a criss-cross, the unbraided wires from the two sides of the loop should mesh together like this, passing between the opposite wires.

Now alternate beaded braids with plain braids on both sets of wires until you have made a total of three pairs of beads on each set of wires. After you have made the last plain braids, join the two sets of wires in a second criss-cross—and you will have completed your first beaded loop. This loop, in the finished watchband, will be left open; it will not be used as a frame for a stone. I call it an "open frame loop."

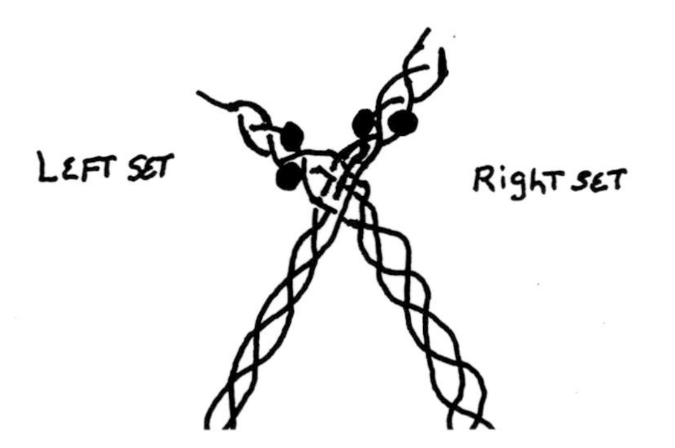

Now you should have a loop of plain braided wire, joined by a criss-cross. Right after the criss-cross, make one very tight braid on the left set of three wires. Continuing to work on the left set, thread a bead onto the left outside wire, and bend it over the center wire; then string a bead on the right outside wire, and bend it over the center wire. Next, make another plain braid, without frame beads. There should now be one very tight braid, one beaded braid, and one plain braid on the left set of wires. Do the same thing on the right set of wires.

You will need to make three more beaded loops, in the same fashion. The first of these *will* be used to frame a stone; I call it a "stone frame loop." The next will be an open frame loop, and the last will be another stone frame loop. This illustration shows the first plain braided loop, the first beaded open frame loop, and the first stone frame loop.

If you used 14 inch wires to make a watchband for a bigger wrist, add an extra full braid to your open loop at each of the points indicated by an arrow above.

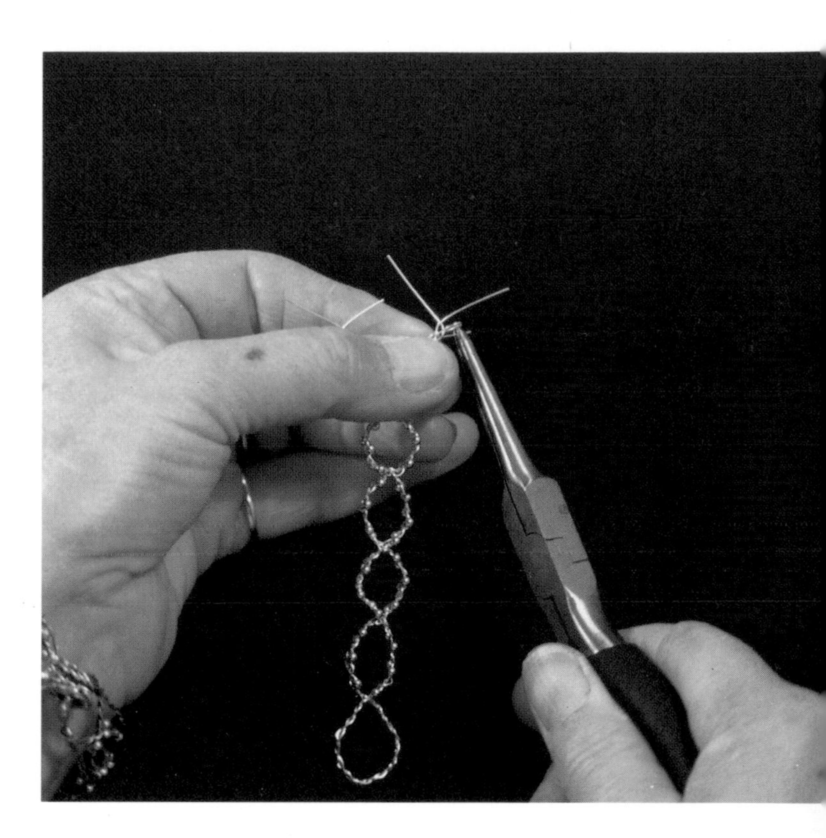

After you have finished the fourth braided loop and the following criss-cross, make one very tight braid in each set of wires. Then braid in one pair of beads (first stringing the bead on the outside wire, then on the inside wire) on each set of wires. Follow each bead pair with seven plain braids.

Holding the watchband half, cut and tuck each braid's outside wires back into the braid, using the pliers. Do not cut or tuck the center wires.

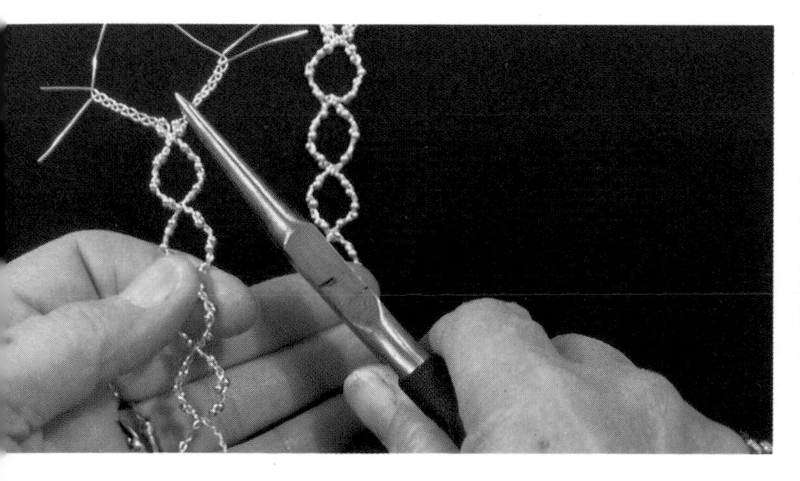

Using the pliers, twist the each of these braids a half-turn, so that the high beads face inside.

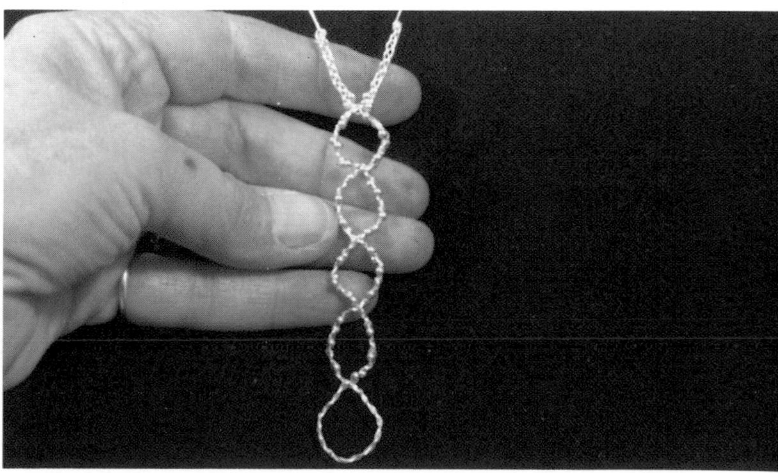

Your band should look like this. All the loops—the first unbeaded loop, the beaded open frame loops, and the beaded stone loops (still empty at this point)—are finished.

Here are the stones resting in their frames. Remember that this is only one half of the watchband; you must make another, identical one to complete the project.

Making the Outside Band Frame

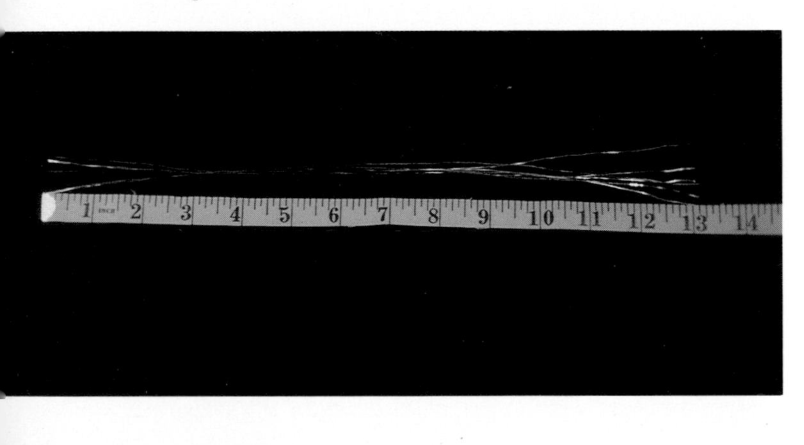

The outside gold frame of your watchband is made from six strands of 24 gauge gold wire, each 13 inches long (or 14 inches for a larger wrist).

Divide the wires into two bundles of three wires in each. Lay the wires side by side, with the ends even. Measure in to the center, and tape them together at this point.

Starting at the center point, make four plain braids in the gold wire. Remove the tape, turn the piece around, and make four more plain braids in the other direction, starting at the center point. You should now have eight braids in the segment. Remember that this will need to be done for two separate bundles of wires, as shown here, one for the border of each half of the watchband. Work with one bundle of wires at a time, alternating from one to the other to complete each set.

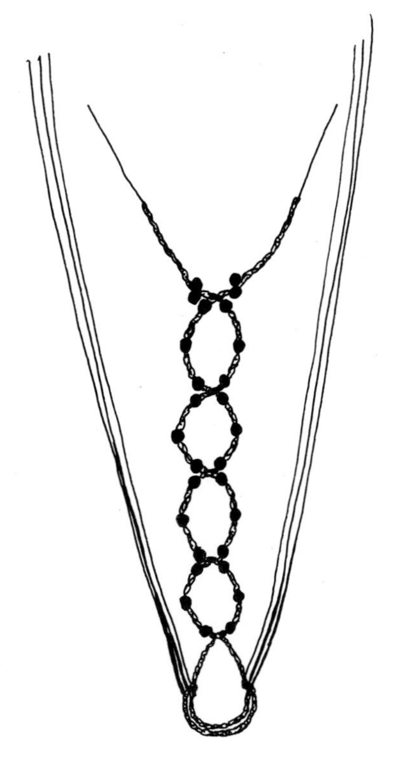

Next, center the braided portion of the gold wire bundle on the end of the silver inside band's first (unbeaded) loop. Bend the gold bundle around the curve of this silver frame. The four plain gold braids on each side should come halfway up the silver frame loop, with the two braids touching. If they do not, add more braids on each side of the gold wire until they do.

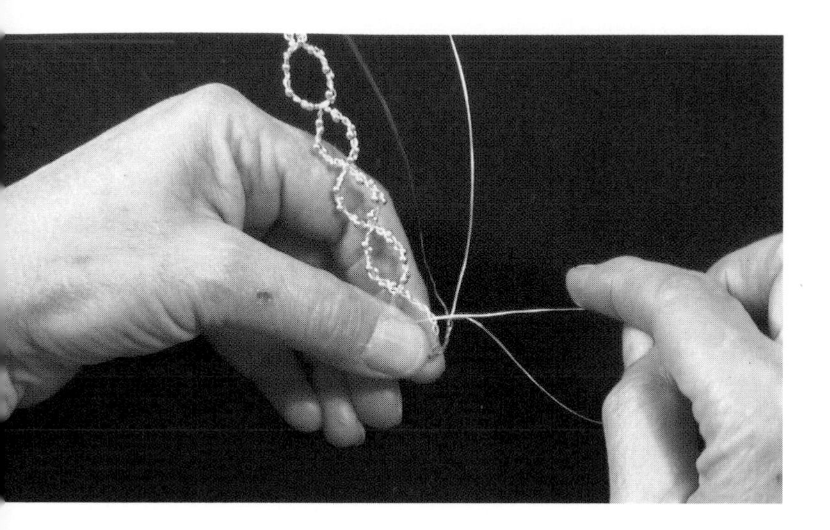

To fasten the two components of the band together, insert the low wire from the gold braid in a corresponding opening in the silver loop, and the high wire in another. (The 'low wire' is the first wire you moved to make the braid; the 'high wire' is the second.) The gold braid's center wire does not get pushed through the silver loop; it should simply be held outside of the frame loop.

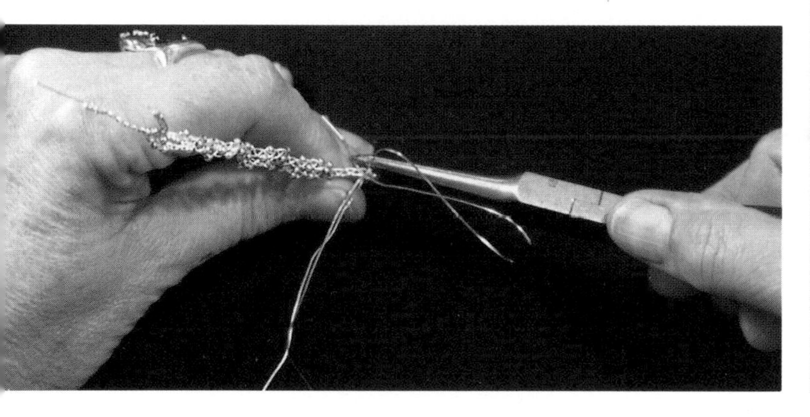

To resume braiding, you will need to 'roll' the high and low gold wires back out of the silver frame loop area.

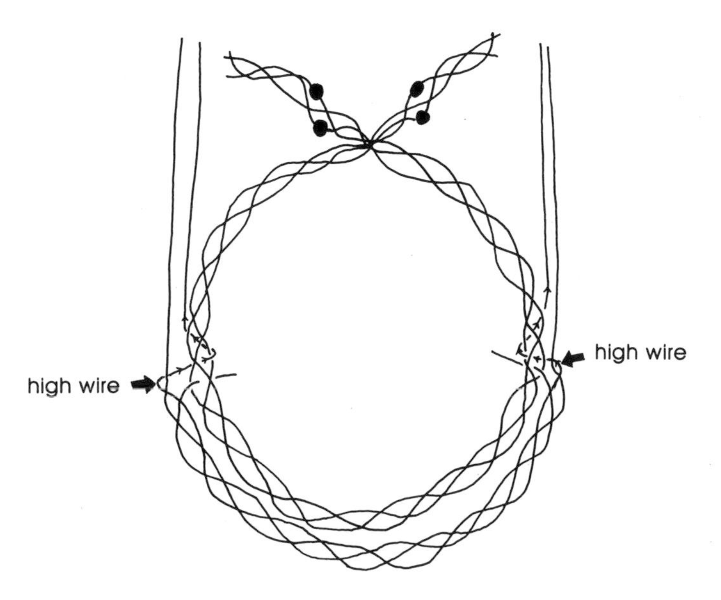

The high wire should be rolled out *underneath* the frame, as shown here.

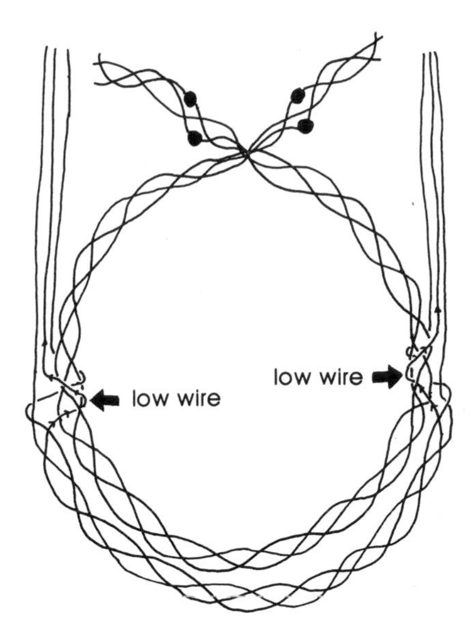

The low wire should be rolled out *over* the frame, as shown here. Before you begin braiding again, pull all of these wires snug.

Now you can resume braiding the gold border wires. Continue braiding each side until the gold braid reaches the midpoints of the first beaded stone frame.

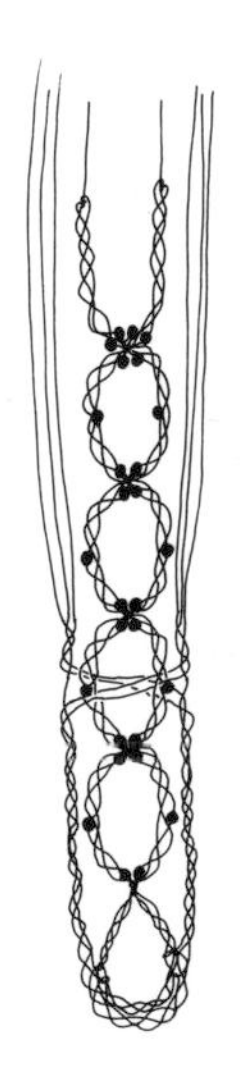

Now you can stretch the still-unbraided length of gold wire across the beaded stone frame to make a backing for the stone, which will end up looking like this.

Working first from the right side, pass the two outside gold wires through two separate openings in the silver beaded frame, at the midpoint of the frame. The center wire stays to the outside.

Stretch the two wires across the frame, and out through openings in the opposite (left) side.

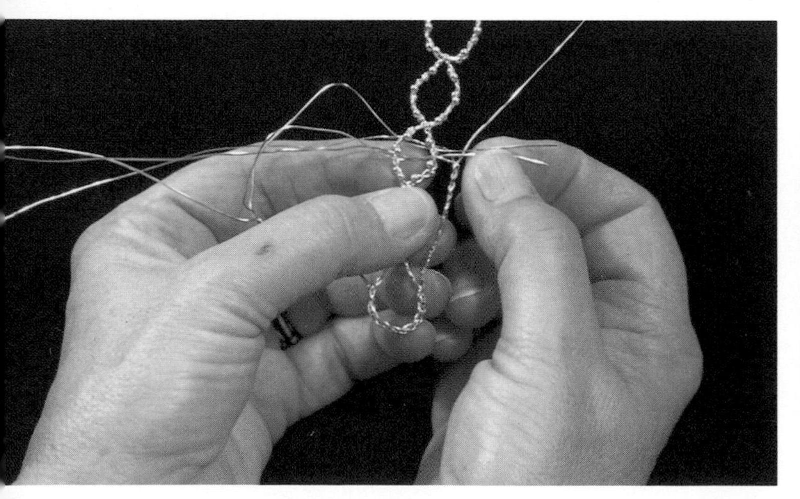

Repeat this process with the braid beginning on the left side. Thread the outside wires in through openings at the midpoint of the beaded frame braid, stretch them across the frame, and then thread them out through openings in the right side of the beaded frame braid.

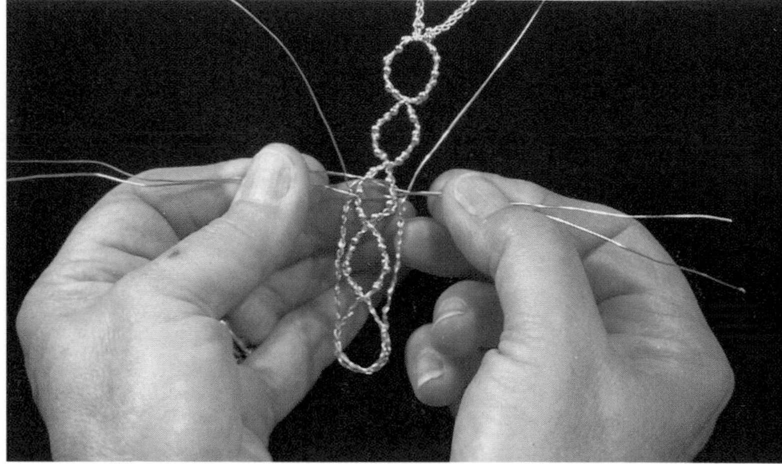

Pull the backing wires tight.

Push the stone into the stone frame until it is seated properly.

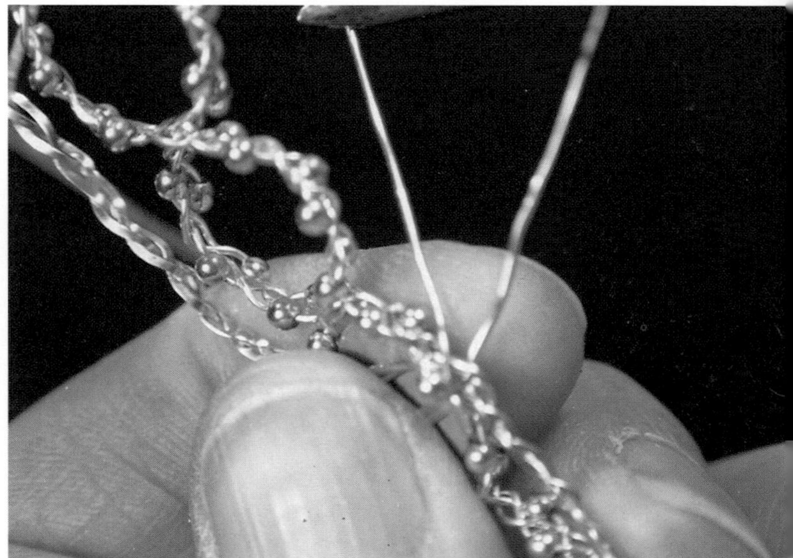

Now you can pull the backing wires as snug as possible, without having to worry about making the frame too small for the stone.

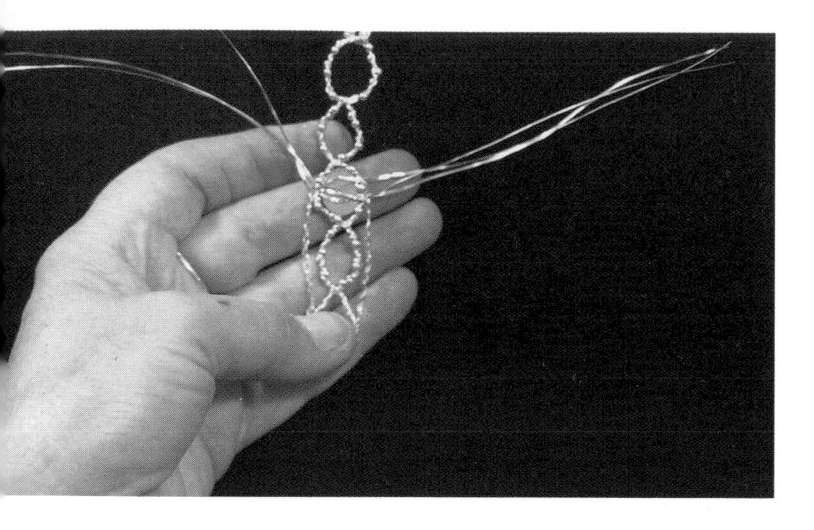

Here is a back view of the band, with four backing wires supporting the stone, and three plain wires on each side ready to resume braiding.

Don't forget that the first loop you pass is merely an open frame loop, not a stone frame. Braid past it.

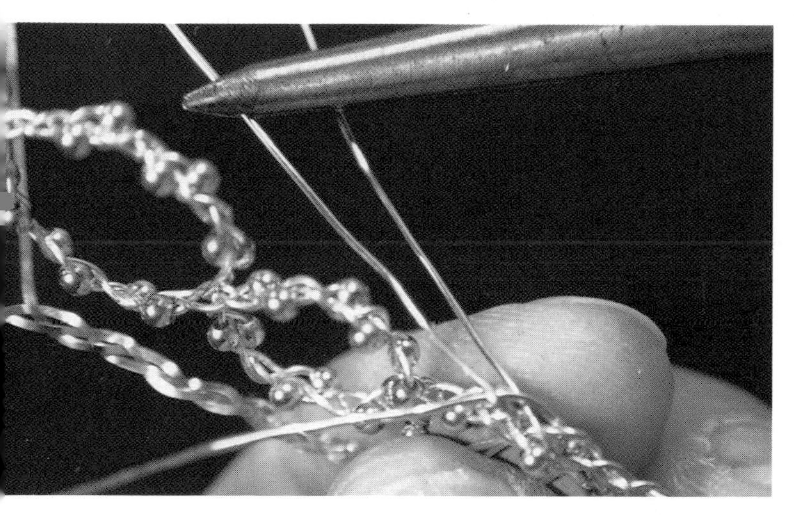

Leaving the stone in place, begin braiding these three wires.

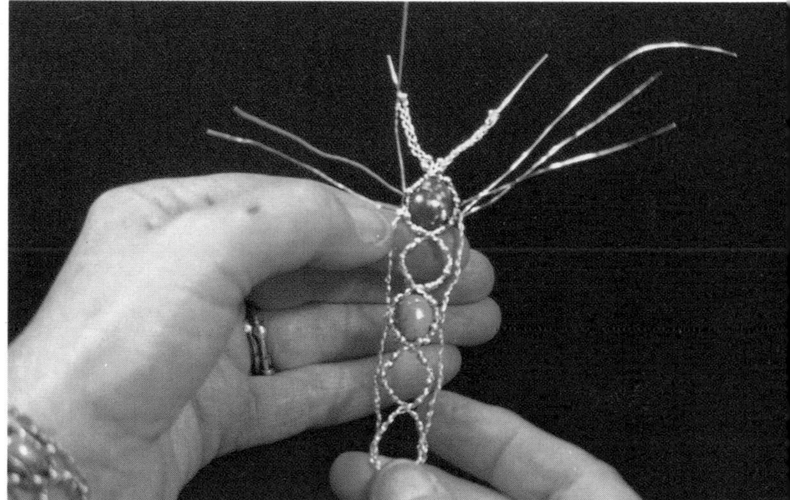

When your gold braids reach the midpoints of the second stone frame, thread the outside wires through the frame as you did before, to make backing wires for the second stone. Put the stone in place, and tighten up the wires.

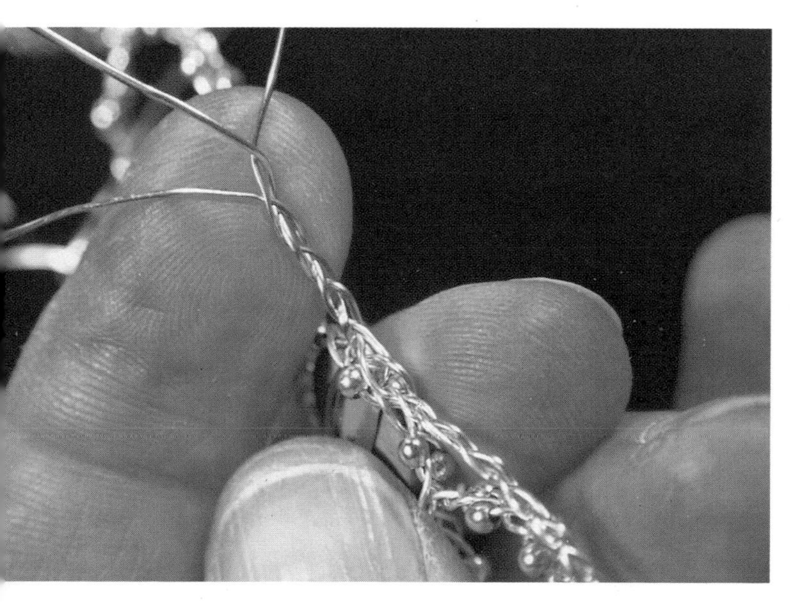

Like before, continue until you reach the middle of the next beaded stone frame.

Braid the loose gold wires on both sides until the braiding is even with the silver braiding of the inside band. Remember to follow all of these steps to finish the second half of the watchband.

Attaching the Watch Face

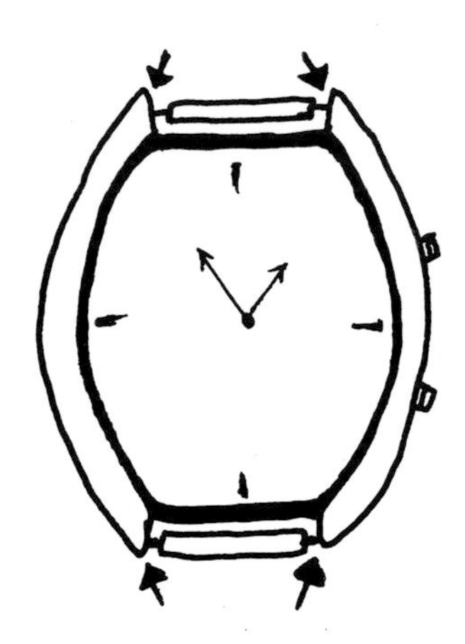

Your watchface will look something like this. The arrows indicate the watch 'ears', which have grooves that fit the pins of the slide pin bar.

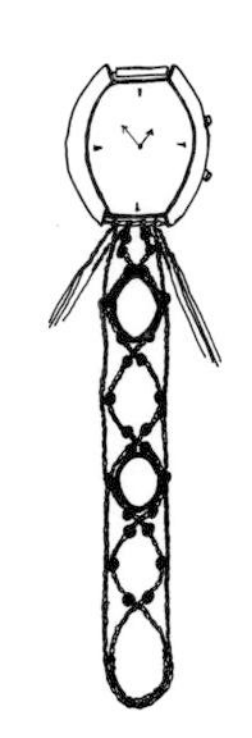

front of watch & band

Push the four braids left dangling from the band between the watch face and the slide pin bar. Be careful your stones do not fall out of place.

This is a slide pin bar. It is a tube with a spring inside, and with pins on the ends to attach it to the ears of the watch face.

If the braided wires are too bulky to fit behind the slide pin bar, gently flatten the braids with your pliers.

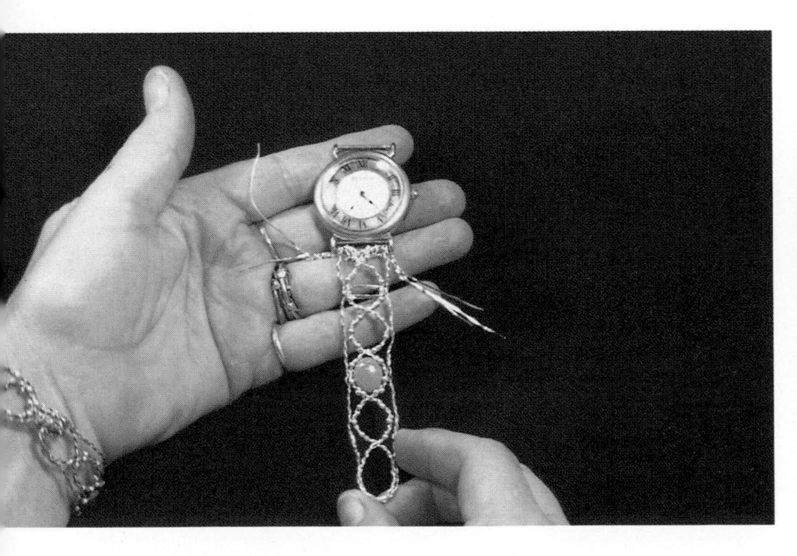

Now you are ready to attach the watchface to the first half of the watchband. Hold the face in one hand and the band in the other, with the front sides up.

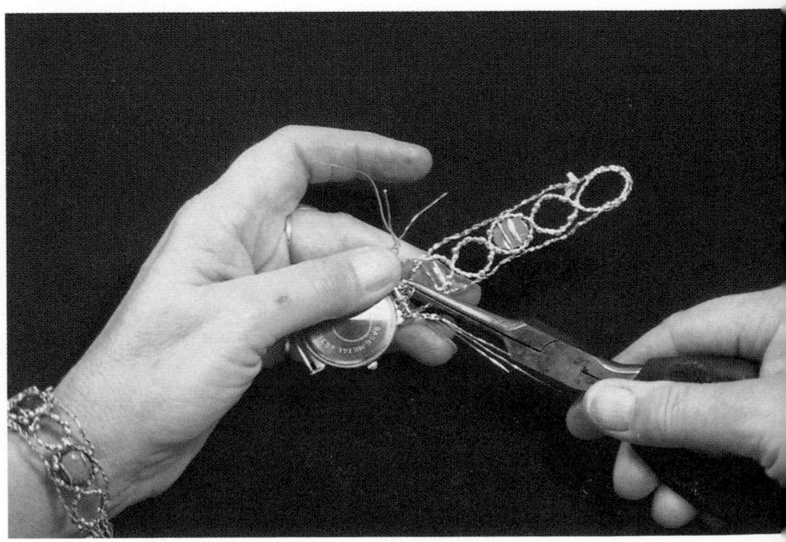

Once the wires are through the opening, bend them backwards until they touch the band frame.

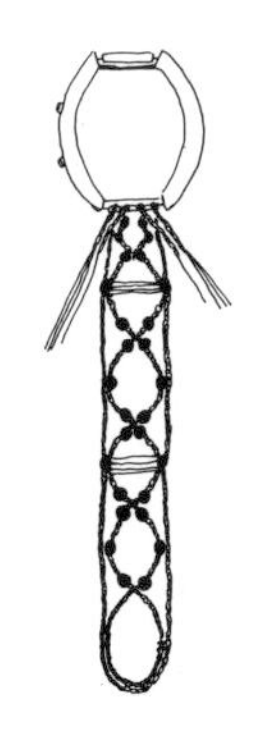

back of watch

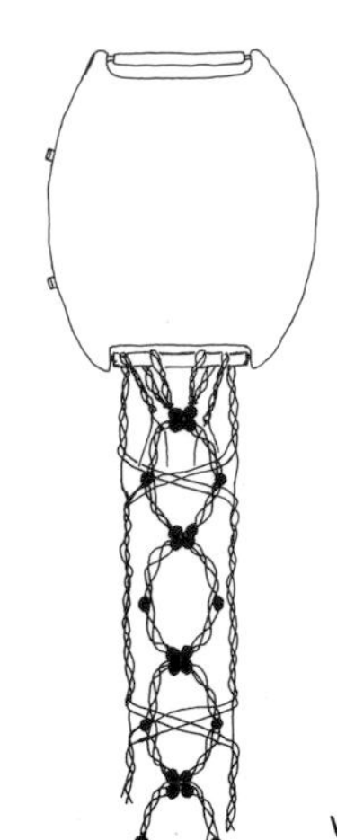

back of watch with retainer started

The last frame beads should be just below the slide pin bar. This is a back view of the watch, showing the back retaining wires. Note that the silver wire braids from the inside of the band have only *one* trailing wire apiece, since their outer wires were cut and tucked away earlier.

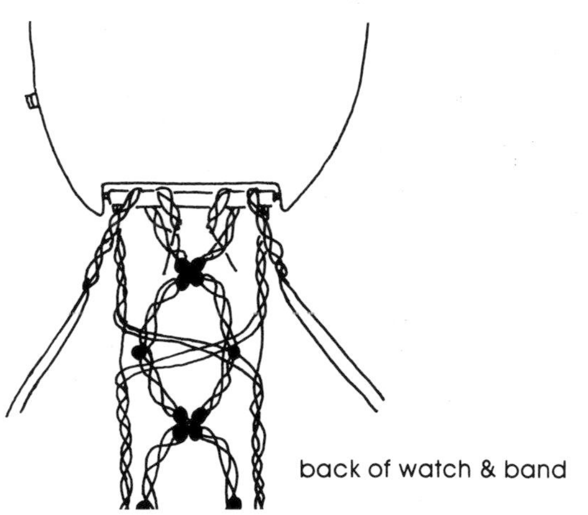

back of watch & band

Push these trailing silver middle wires through the openings they touch in their braided segments.

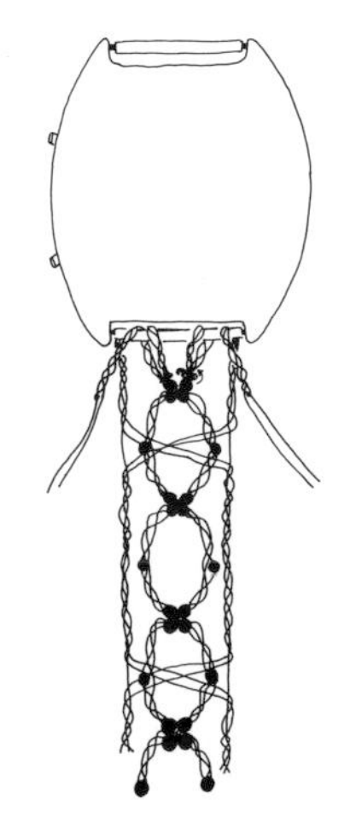

Make two or three wraps; then cut and tuck the wires out of sight.

Next, bend the gold braids of the outside frame so that they are even with the top of the inside stone frame wires on the back side.

Cut one wire of each braid...

...and tuck it out of sight. Save the scrap wire lengths; if they are long enough, you may be able to use them in the next instruction (see the second paragraph).

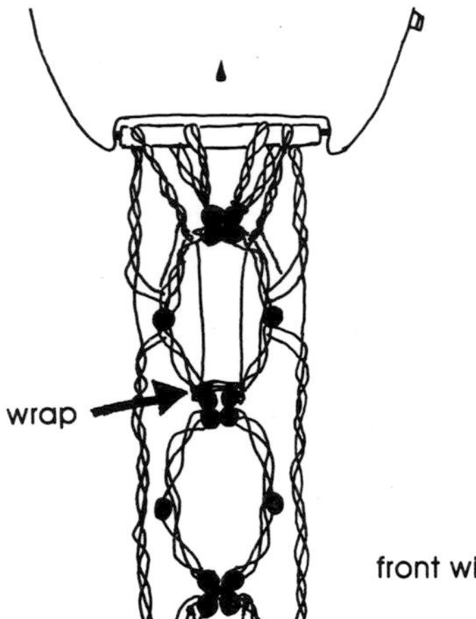

Take each of the middle wires (now at the back of the band) and push them through the stone frame right next to the framing beads on their respective sides. Then run these middle wires over the top of the stone, along each side. Next, push the wires through the frame at the base of the stone. If the wires are long enough, make one wrap (tightly) around the base of the stone frame, between the beaded open loop and the stone frame as shown. Cut any excess wire and tuck the ends out of sight.

Next, cut two pieces of wire the correct length to make retainers for the other stone frame. (You may be able to use the two scrap lengths of wire cut from the first wire you tucked, in the previous instruction.)

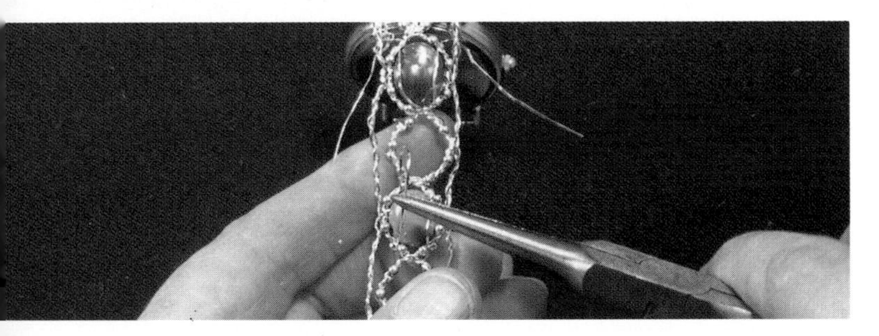

Make a hook in one end of each wire, insert it in the stone frame right next to the top framing bead, and crimp the hook closed. Run the wires over the top of the stone along the sides, out through the frame at the other end.

Then cut and tuck the ends out of sight.

There should now be one loose wire on each side of the band.

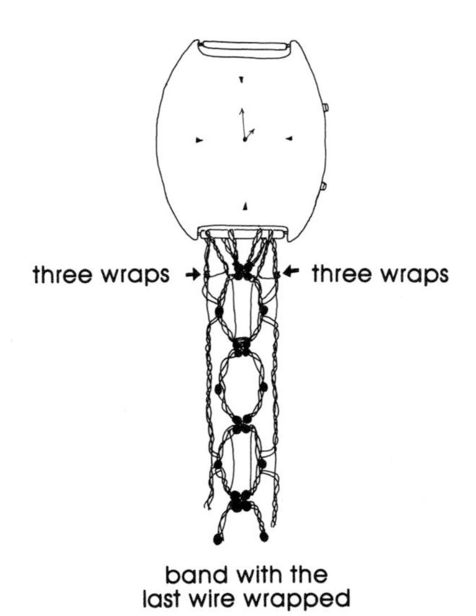

band with the last wire wrapped

Pull these over to the outer frame, as shown, and make three wraps.

Cut and tuck the wire out of sight. Now one side of your band is securely fastened to the watchface. Repeat these steps to attach the second side of the band.

Making the Hook

Once both halves of the watchband have been made and attached to the watchface, the hook has to be shaped. Place the watch on your wrist the way you would wear it. The section of the band that is closest to your body will have the hook part of the clasp; the last loop on the other side will serve as a catch. Grasp the hook side of the band in one hand and use the pliers to gently squeeze the final loop together to about half its original width.

Place this narrow loop between the jaws of the pliers at the middle of the loop, and bend it almost double.

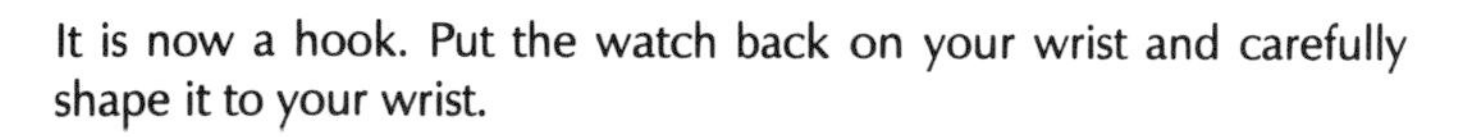

It is now a hook. Put the watch back on your wrist and carefully shape it to your wrist.

Bend the hook loop slightly upward at the tip so that it can catch the last loop of the other side more easily.

Securing the Stones

To finish this project, make sure that the stones are straight and properly seated in their frames. Mix a small amount of epoxy glue and put a thin layer on the back of the stones and the backing wires. For the best results, let the glue set for 48 hours before moving the watch.

Here is the finished watch. If the band is a little too large, just spread the open beaded loops wider to take up some of the length; if the band is a little too small, pinch them to be narrower (like the hook) to add some length. This is the reason it is important to leave some open loops in the first place!

Project #7

BUTTERFLY

Necklace & Earrings

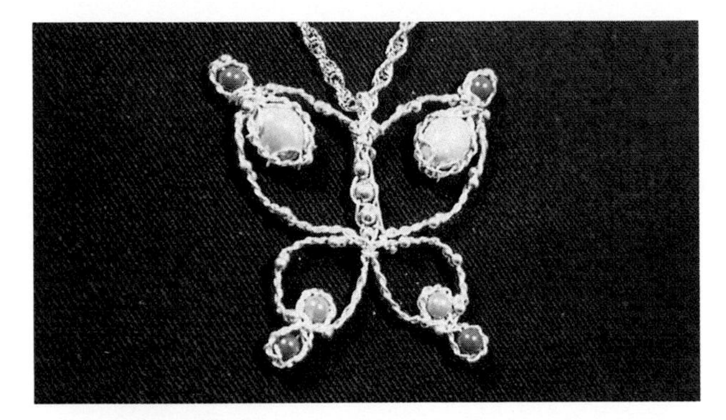

MATERIALS

24 gauge silver or gold wire
one 3 mm silver or gold bead (for body)
one 4 mm silver or gold bead (for body)
2 mm gold or silver beads (for body and frame)
Two 8 x 10 mm oval stones
Four 3 mm garnet beads
Two 3 mm turquoise beads
Two 4mm or 6 mm turquoise beads

TOOLS

ruler
epoxy glue
masking tape
needle or pin
scissors or wire cutters
smooth-jawed needle-nose pliers

Making the Body

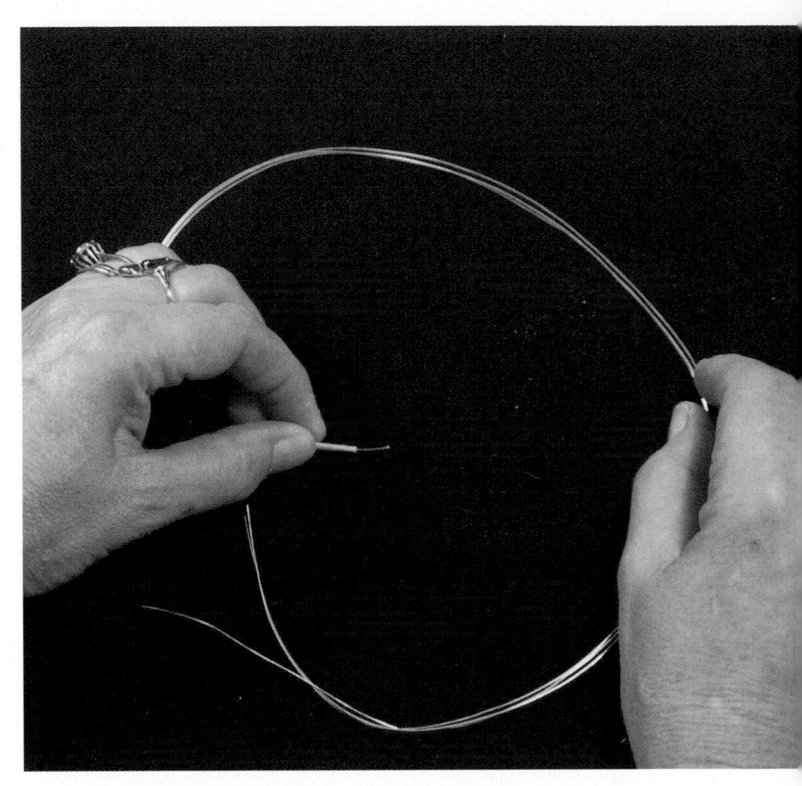

Measure and cut three pieces of 24 gauge silver wire, each 22 inches long. Hold the wires side by side with the ends even, and tape the bundle about 1 inch from the top.

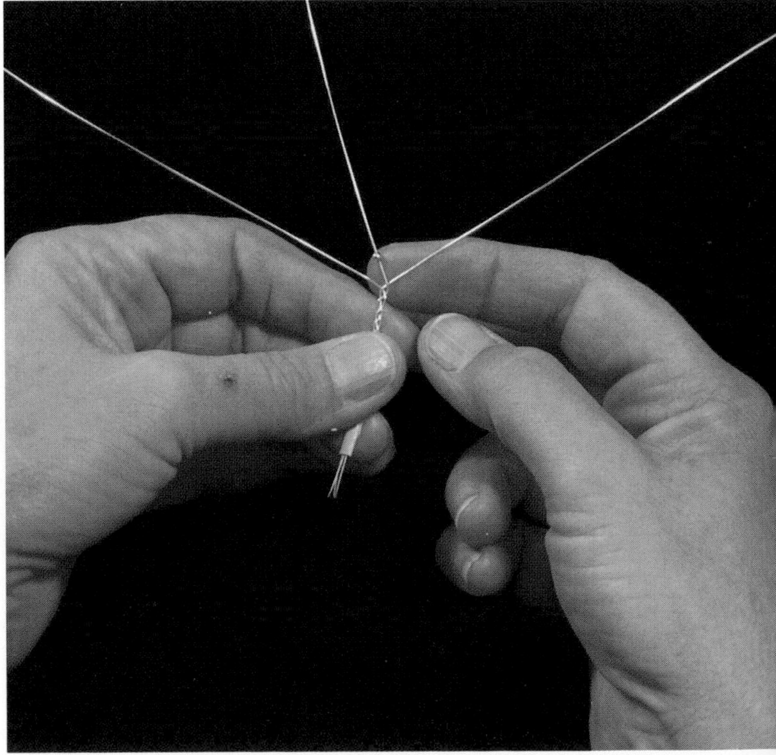

Make eight braids from the tape. These initial plain braids will be used to make a chain loop later. Then put one 3 mm gold bead on the center wire and braid it in with one plain braid

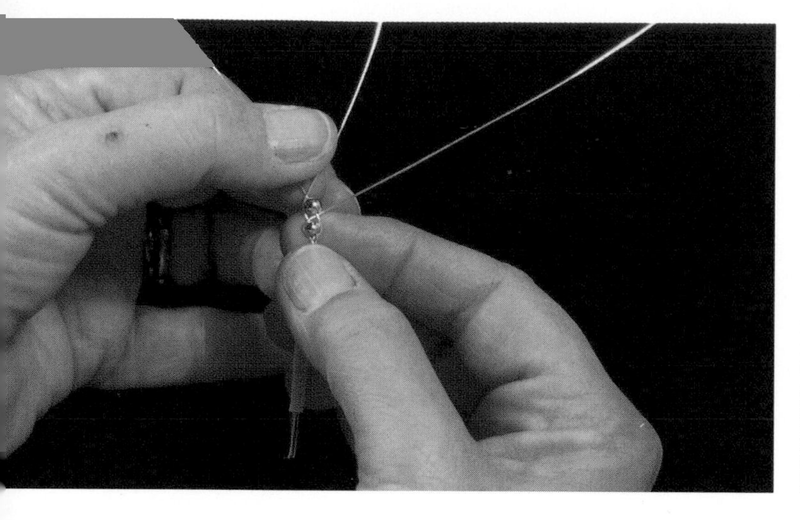

Then add one 4 mm gold bead on the center wire and braid it in with one plain braid.

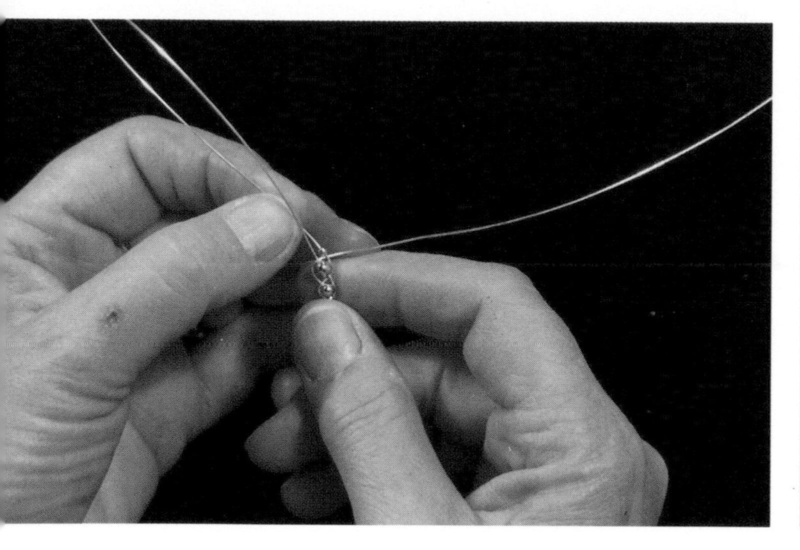

Then add one 2 mm gold bead on the center wire and braid it in with one plain braid.

Your piece should now look like this.

Making the Lower Wings

Make eight braids from the 2 mm body bead.

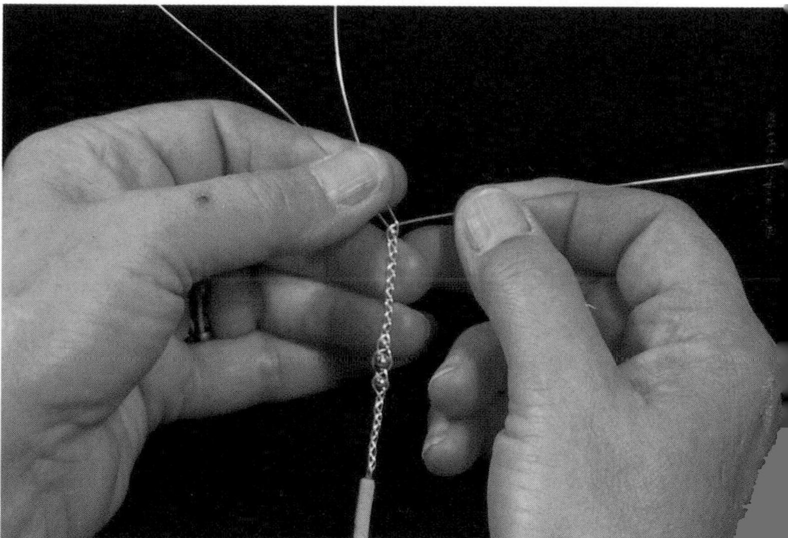

Then put one 2 mm frame bead on the center wire...

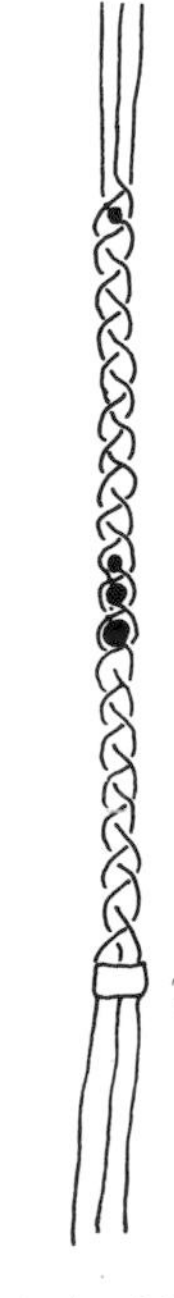

...and braid it in with one plain braid.

Then braid another eight braids.

Your piece should look like this.

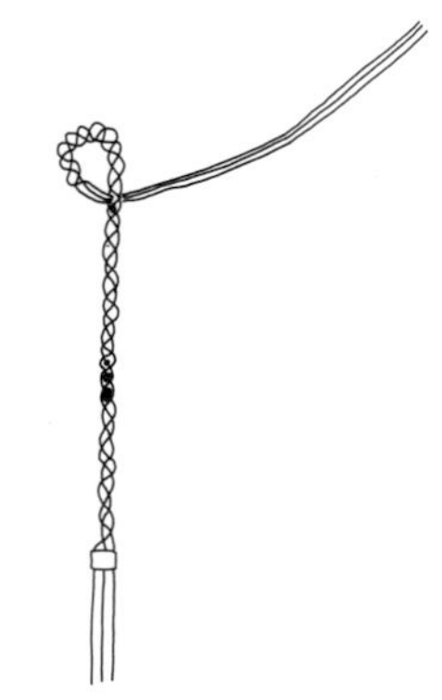

Next, pass all three unbraided wires through an opening in front of the 2 mm frame bead.

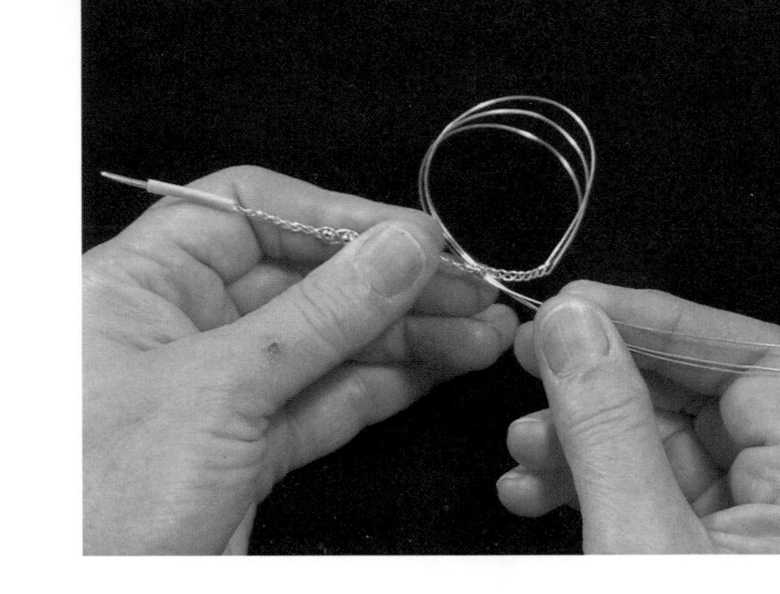

Gently pull the wire through, alternating from one wire to the other...

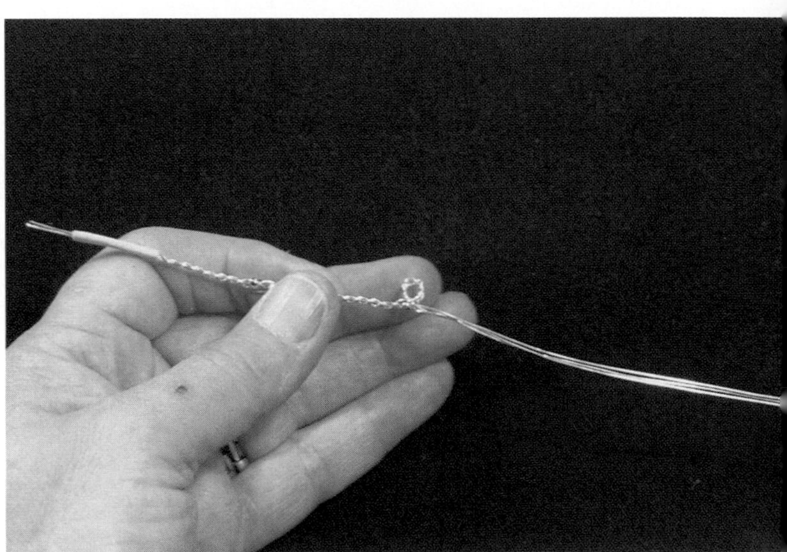

...until they are snug. The last braid must be flush against the existing braided wire. This is the first of eight small loops in this project, which will serve as bead frames for colored stones. The one I just made will be one of the six smallest, which will frame stone beads. Two slightly larger small loops will be used as frames for oval flat-backed stones on the insides of the top wings.

Braid nine more braids.

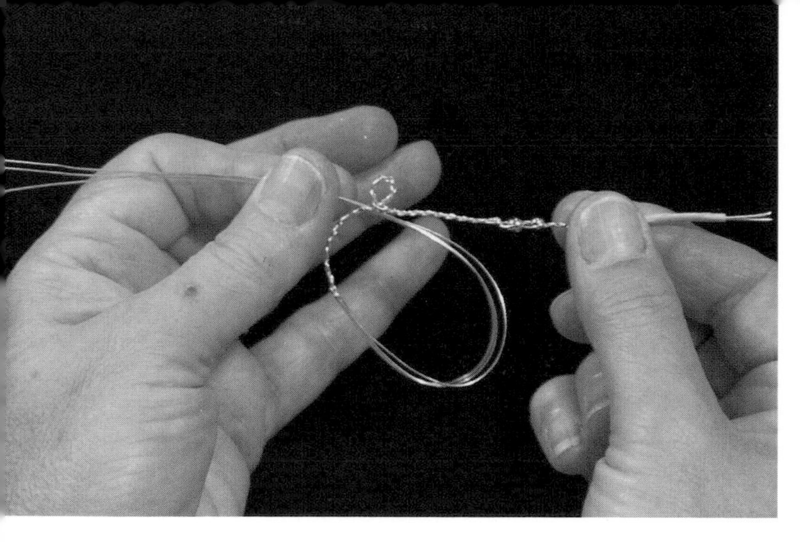

Then bend the wire in a loop backwards, towards the taped end of the wire bundle. Pass the unbraided ends of the wire through a single opening in the first of the new nine braids. The loose ends should now be pointing *away* from the taped end.

Again, be sure that the last braid is snug and flush with the previously braided wire.

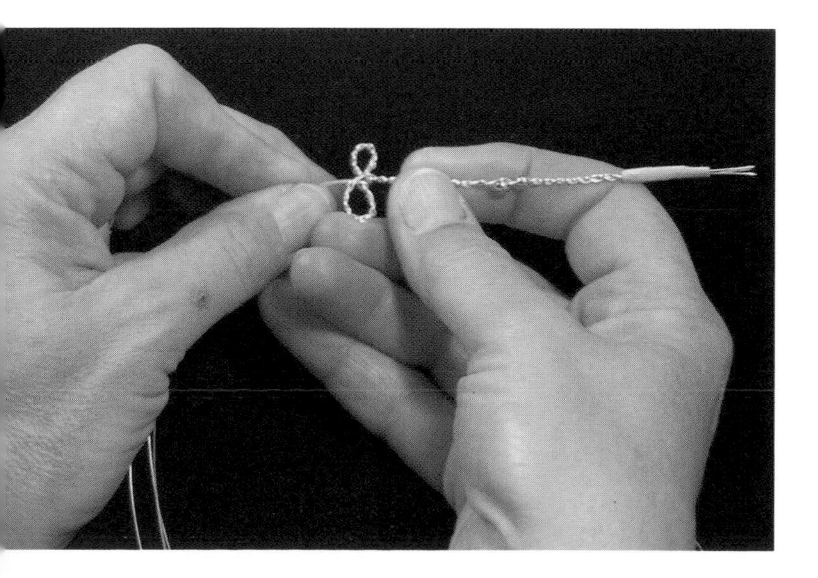

You should now have two small frame loops at the end of the braided portion of your wire bundle.

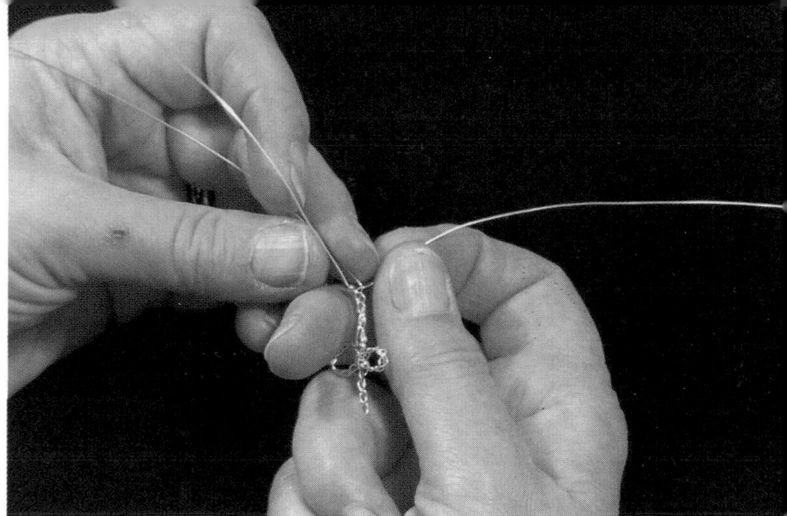

From here, you will continue your braid in a double-sided frame bead pattern. Start right after the two small frame loops, and add one 2 mm gold bead on the left outside wire; then cross that wire over the center wire ('braiding it in'). Next add a 2 mm bead to the right outside wire, and braid *that* wire in. Make four plain braids, and add another pair of beads. In this photo, I am adding the lefthand bead of the second bead set. Then I will braid it in by crossing the left wire over the center wire.

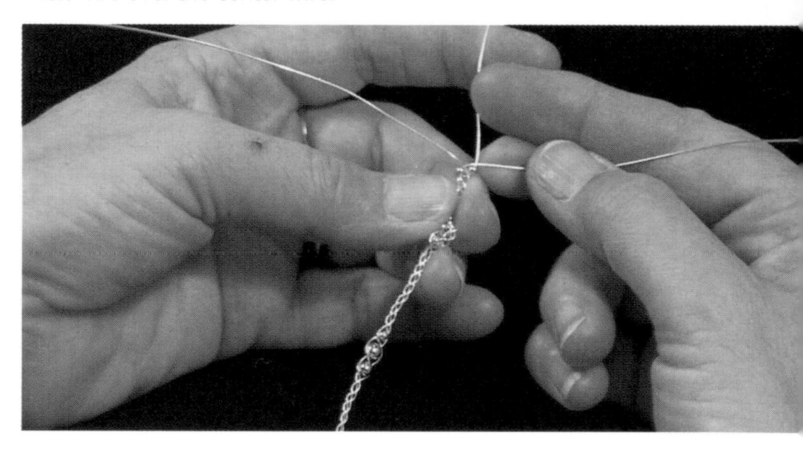

Then add the righthand bead, and braid it in.

Make another four plain braids, and braid in the final set of beads. Then finish off this segment with two plain braids.

Your piece should now look like this.

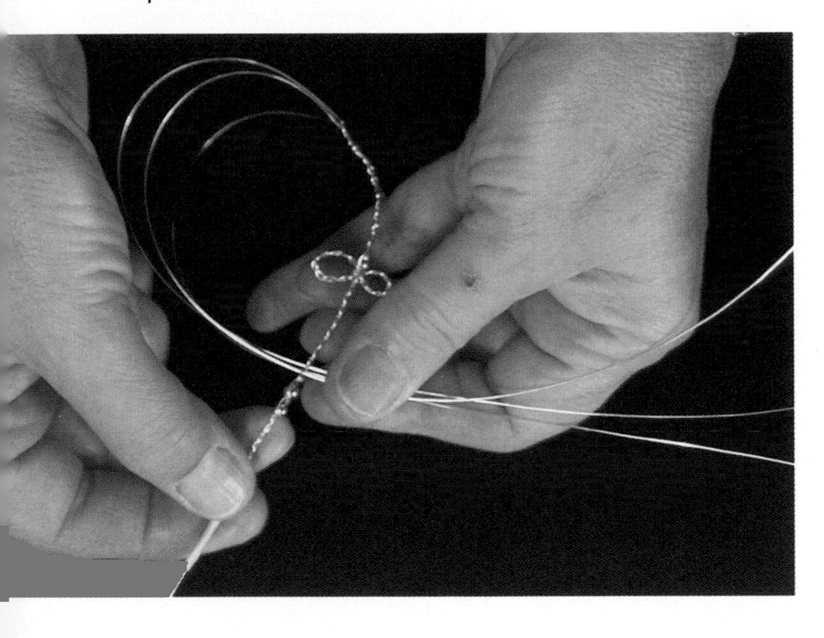

Then pass the wires through a single opening in the frame just below the 2 mm body bead.

Again make sure that the wires are pulled through tightly and are flush. You have now made your first lower wing.

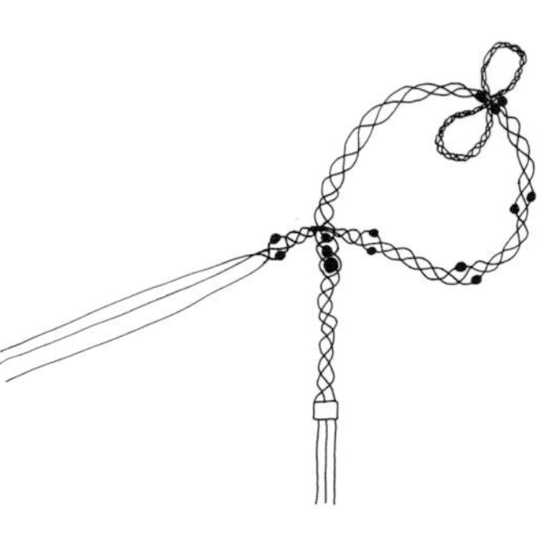

When this first butterfly wing has been pulled snug, it is time begin the second lower butterfly wing. To do this, follow the sam procedure as before—but in reverse. First, make two plain braid then braid in a pair of 2 mm frame beads on the outside wires as yo did for the previous segment.

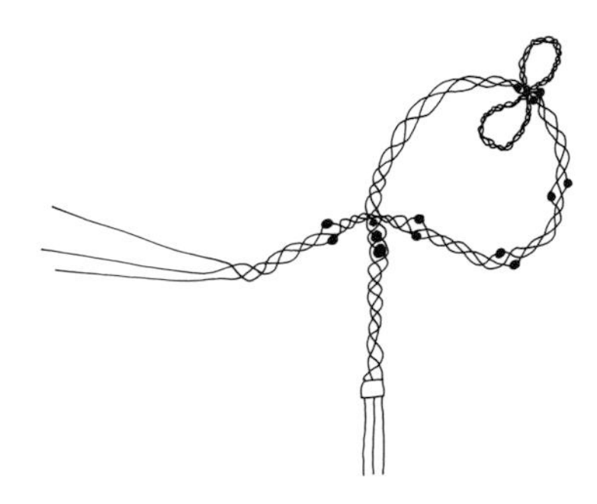

Follow the beads with four plain braids.

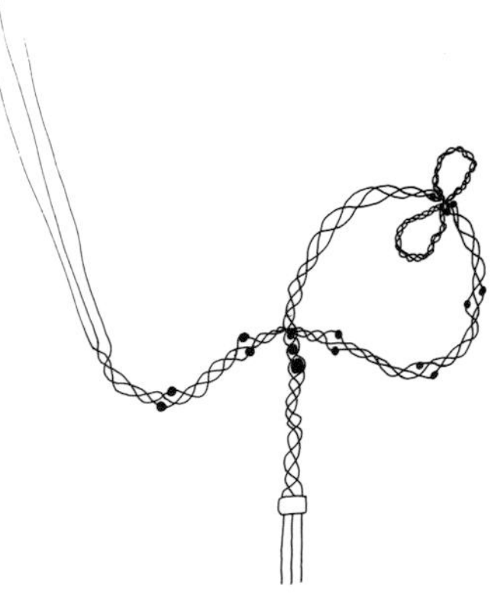

Add another pair of 2 mm frame beads, followed by four plain braid

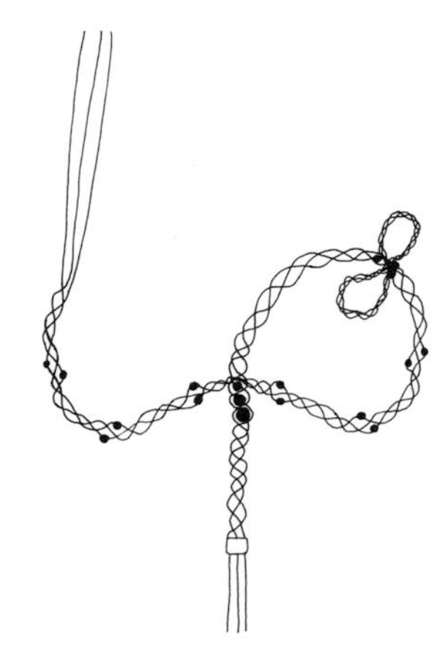

Add another pair of frame beads; then, four plain braids.

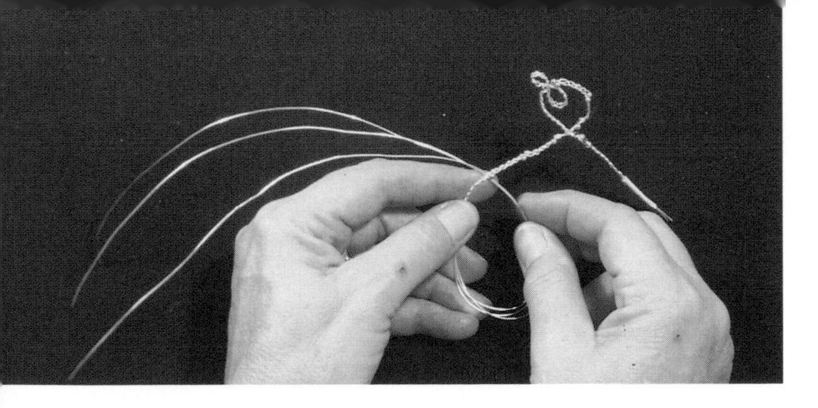

To make the first stone frame loop for your second butterfly wing, braid in a final pair of frame beads. Then make a series of eight plain braids, which will become the loop of the stone frame. Pass the wires through a single opening in front of the last frame beads.

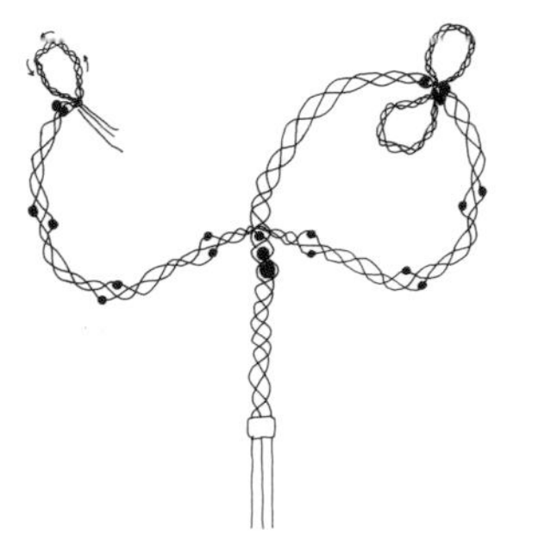

Here you can see in detail the steps neccesary.

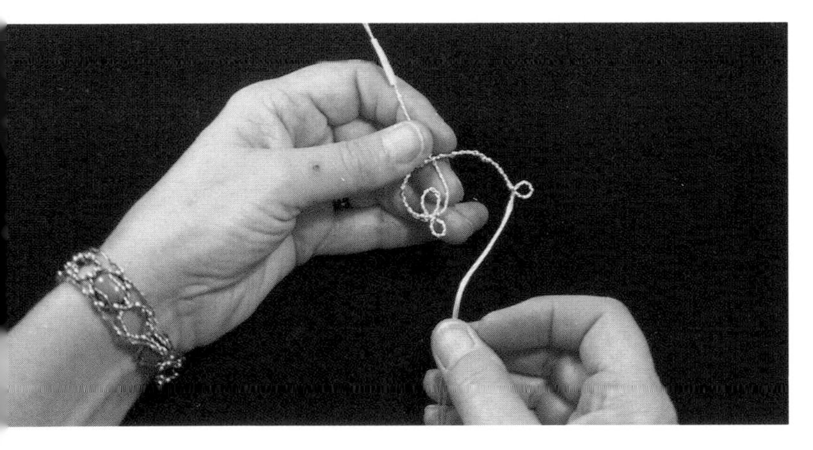

Pull the wires tight and flush. You should now have a small frame loop like the one you made for the first wing.

Make another eight braids, and then pass the loose ends of the wire back through an opening in the first of these braids. Be sure to thread the wires through as shown here, so that after the loop is made, the ends point away from the body of the butterfly.

Pull them flush and tight. Now you should have two small frame loops in a figure-eight shape for the second wing. Add a single 2 mm frame bead on the center wire and braid it in, and then braid eight plain braids.

To make the large loop outlining the second lower wing, pass the wires through an opening beneath the 2 mm body bead, and through to the other side as shown.

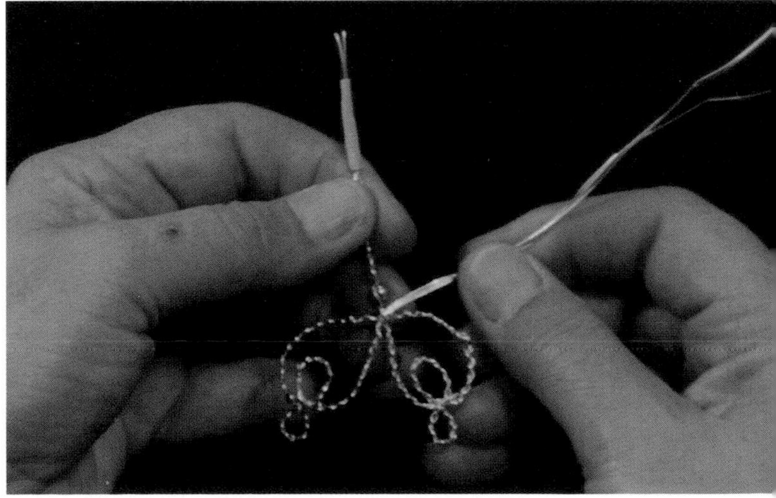

Your butterfly should now look like this, with both lower wings completed. Notice the direction that the body beads are facing.

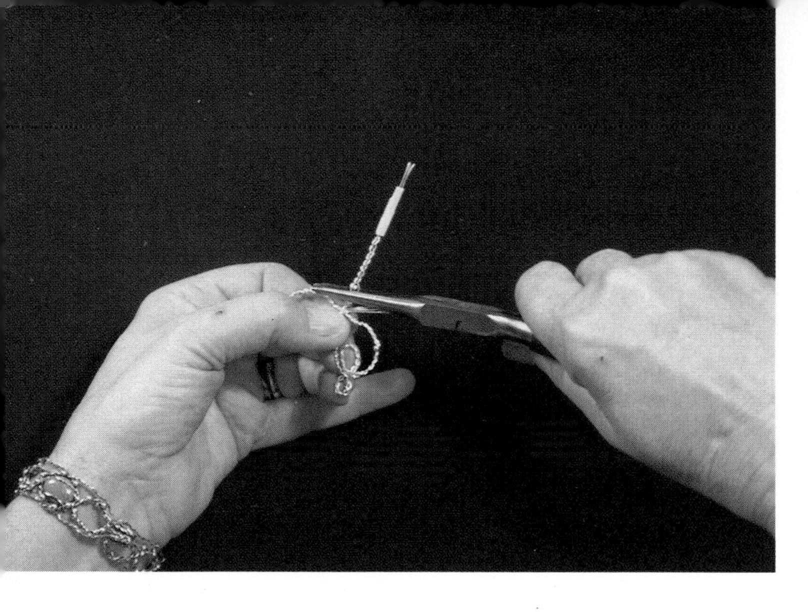

Hold the bottom wings firmly in your fingers. Use the pliers to twist the body beads a half-turn, so that they are facing you. This will also tighten the joint where the wires cross over.

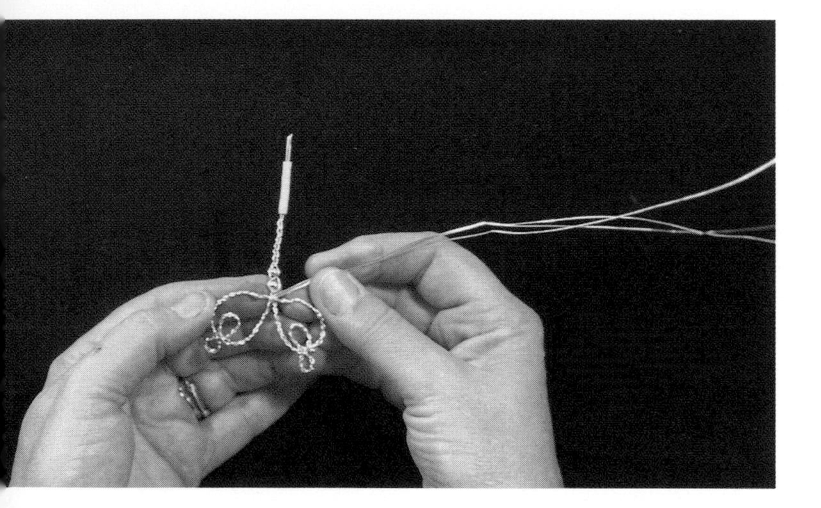

Your butterfly should now look like this. Again, notice the direction of the body beads; now they face you frontways. If you have not done so already, be sure to flip your piece so that the taped ends are at the top, and the completed wings are at the bottom.

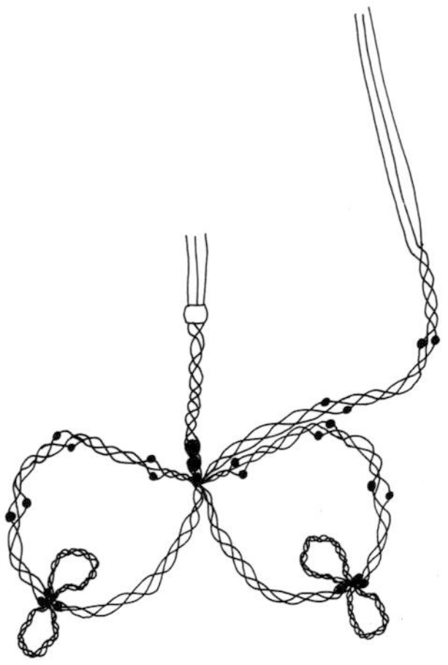

Making the Upper Wings

Now the top portion of the wings will be made. Braid four plain braids.

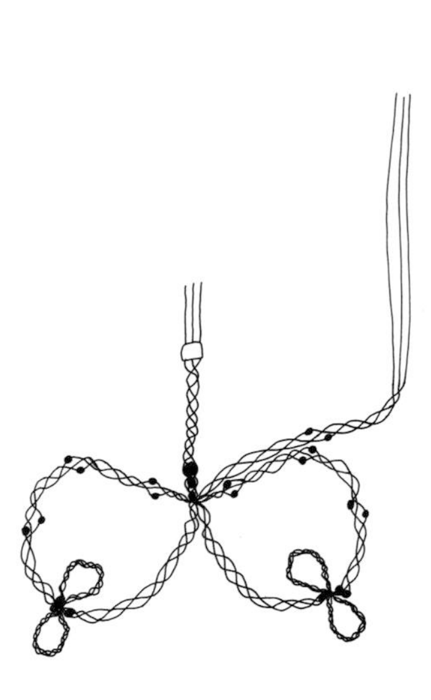

Then braid in one bead on each outside wire, followed by four plain braids.

Repeat this: braid in one bead on each outside wire, and then make four plan braids.

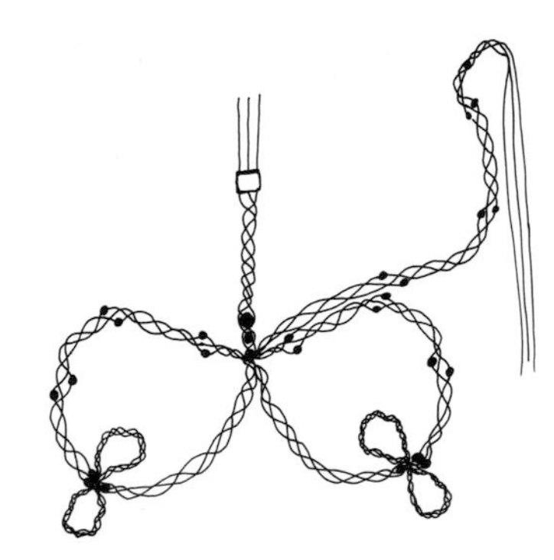

Then another bead on each outside wire, and another four plain braids. There should be three sets of double-sided frame beads, in between sets of four plain braids. Finally, braid in one bead on the center wire, and finish with four plain braids.

To make the first small stone frame loop in the upper wing, push the center wire back through the braid in front of the last set of frame beads.

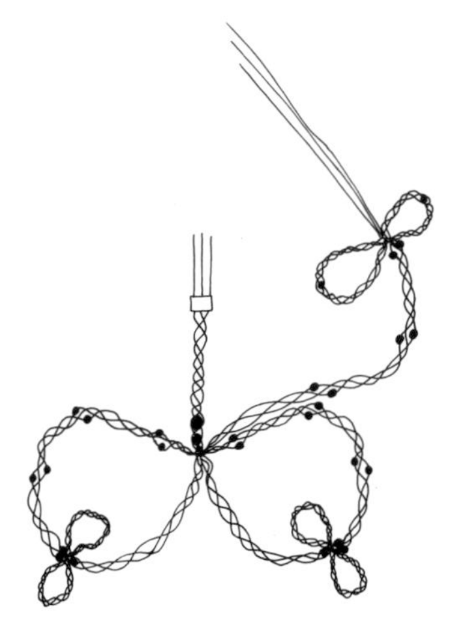

Then braid another 7 1/2 plain braids. To complete the loop, pass the wires through the first braid of this loop, and pull it tight.

Pull the wires tight and flush with the frame. Your first small bead-frame loop (the top of the figure-eight) is done.

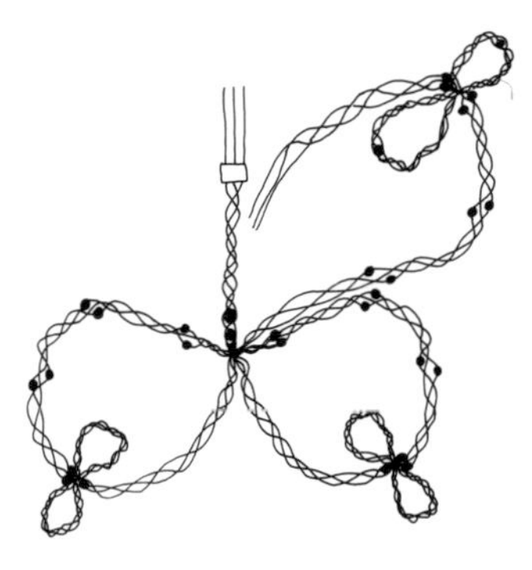

To finish the wing, braid in one 2 mm bead on each outside wire, followed by four plain braids.

The corresponding small loop (the bottom of the figure-eight) is actually a bit bigger. To make this loop, first make 7 1/2 braids. Then thread one bead on the center wire, and braid it in.

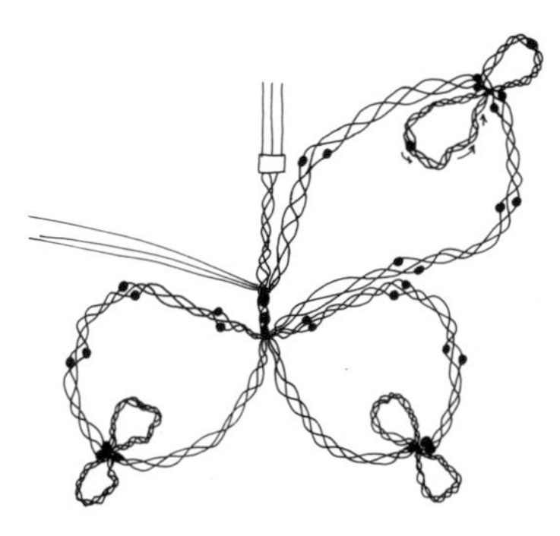

Then braid in one bead on each outside wire again, followed by another four plain braids. Push the wires through the bottom braid of the chain loop just above the 3 mm body bead.

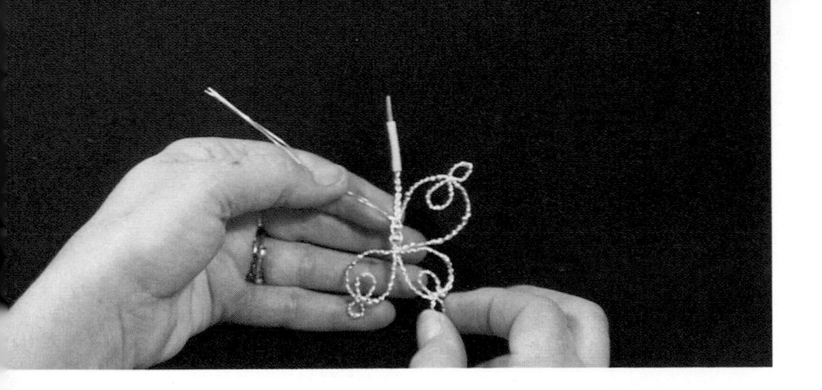

Pull the wires tight and flush with the chain loop braid.

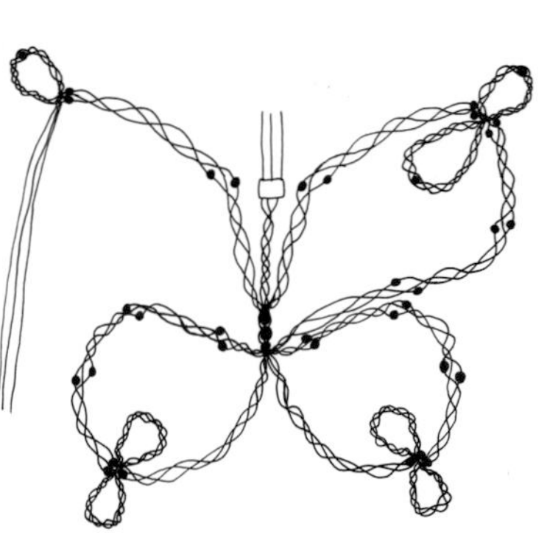

For the small top loop, make four plain braids, add one bead on the center wire, and make another four plain braids. Push the wires through in front of the last bead set, and pull them tight and flush.

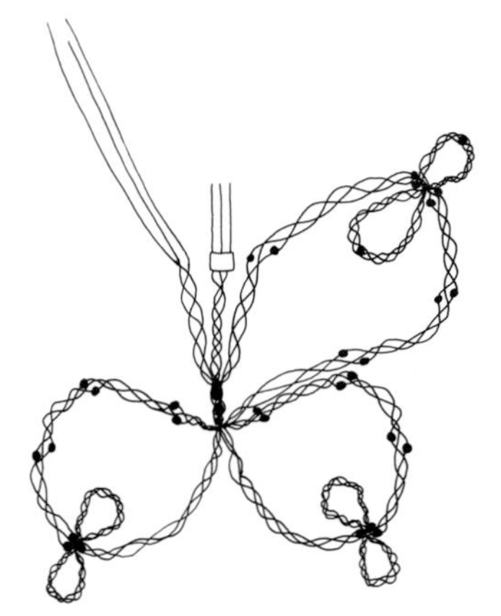

To make the last wing, use the same steps in reverse. First braid four plain braids.

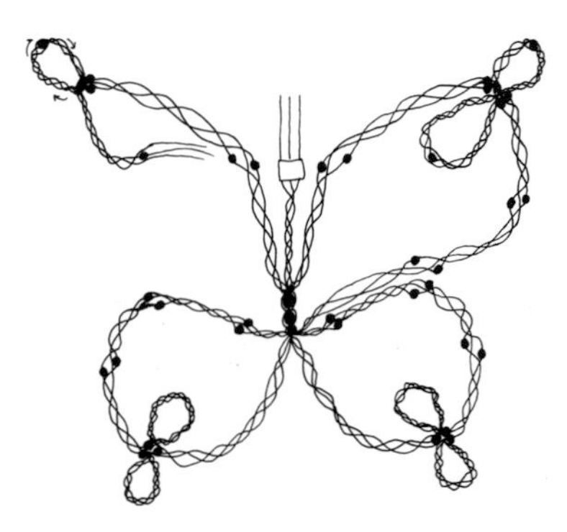

To make the larger of the two small loops, make 7 1/2 plain braids, add one bead on the center wire and braid it in.

Then braid one 2 mm bead on each outside wire, and make another four plain braids.

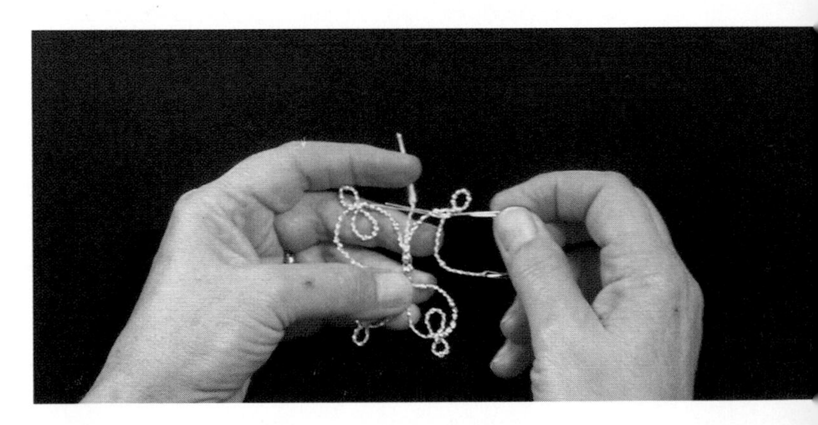

Then braid another set of 7 1/2 plain braids, and push the loose ends of the wires through the first braid in the loop.

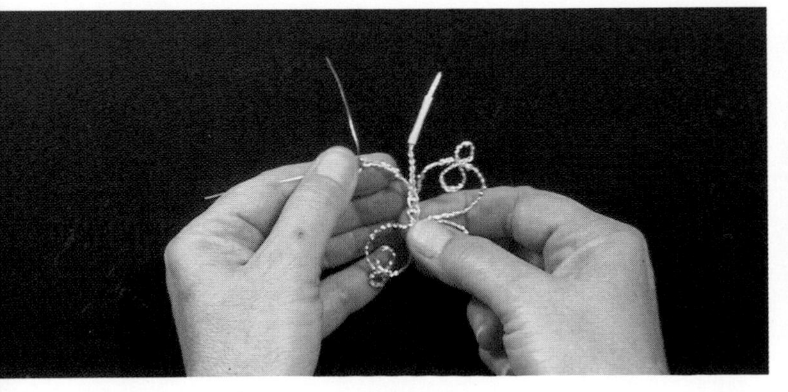

Again, add one bead on each outside wire, and braid them in.

Pull the wires tight.

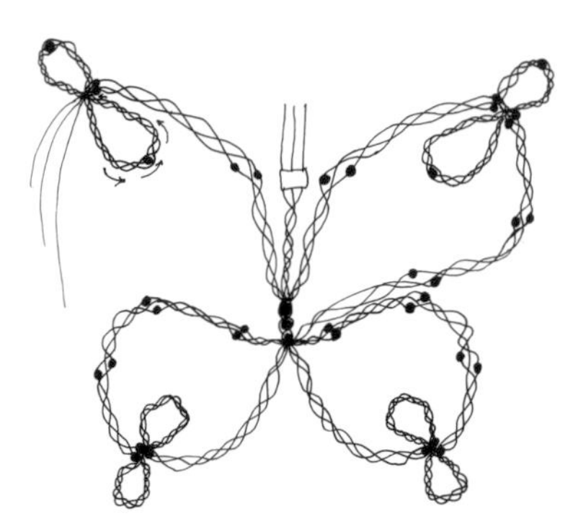

Your butterfly should now look like this.

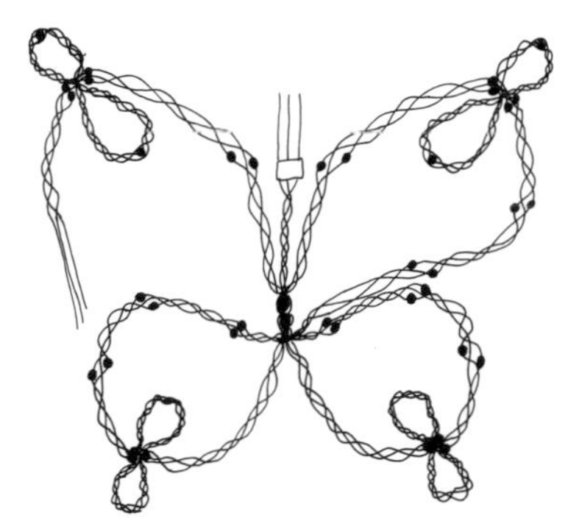

To finish the wing, place one bead on each outside wire and braid it in, and then make four plain braids.

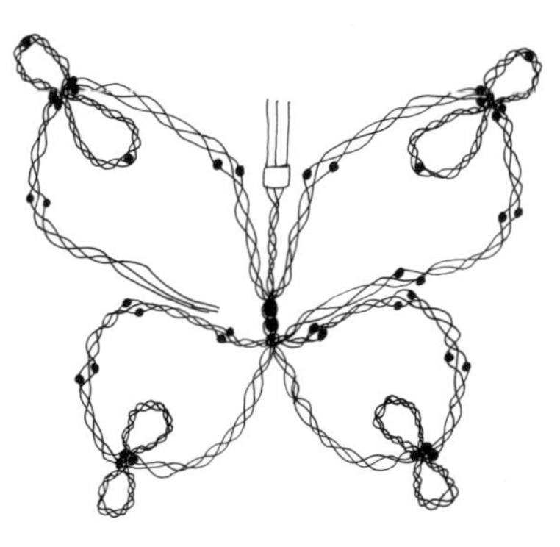

Then add one bead on each outside wire and braid it in, and make another four plain braids.

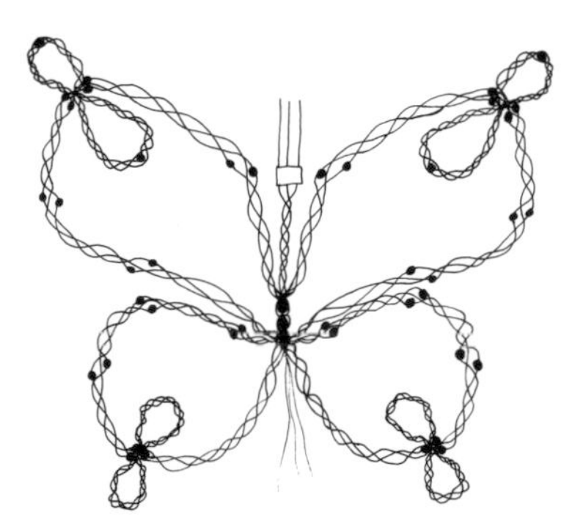

Add another single bead to each outside wire and braid it in, and make a final four plain braids. To fasten the last wing in place, push the wires through the joint between the upper and lower wings, threading them down through and between the lower wings.

Your butterfly should now look like this.

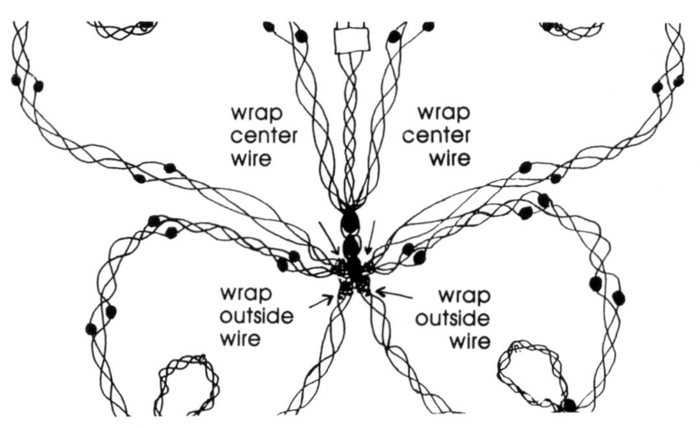

Wrap the outside wires around the lower wings; wrap the center wire first around the right upper wing, then around the left upper wing. Finally, cut and tuck any loose ends.

Adding Stone Beads to the Lower Wings

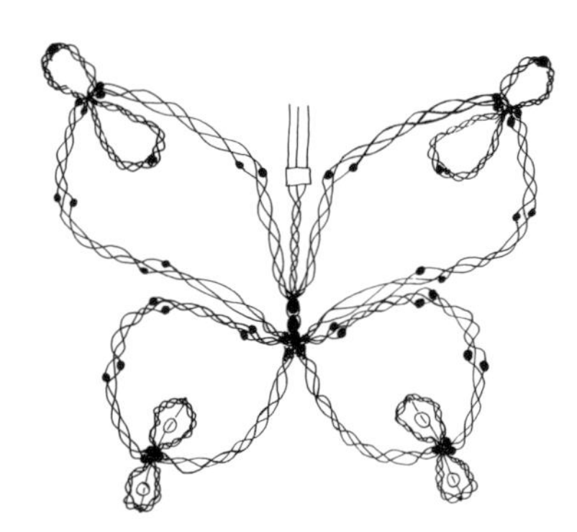

Now the stone beads can be strung into the stone bead frames of the lower wings, as shown here.

Use a nail or something round to shape the frames if they are not circular. Then, to open a path for the bead-stringing wire, run a needle or a pin through the center of the frames—vertically, through the center of the figure-eight, as shown here.

Cut a short segment of beading wire. Crimp one end, run it through the frame and the stone beads, and crimp the other end.

Tuck the ends out of sight. Do both sides the same way.

Adding Stone Beads and Oval Flat-Backed Stones to the Upper Wings

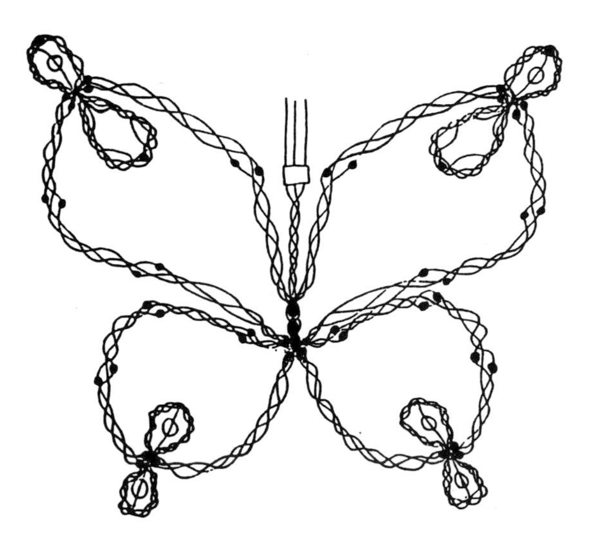

The upper wings have two small loops (for round beads like those used in the the lower wings) and two larger loops (for oval flat-backed stones). The round beads will be strung on a beading wire, like the round beads of the lower wings were. The oval flat-backed stones, however, must be secured with retaining wires, like those used in previous projects.

To start adding stone beads to the first upper wing, use a pin or a needle to open a path for the beading wire and the stone frame retainers.

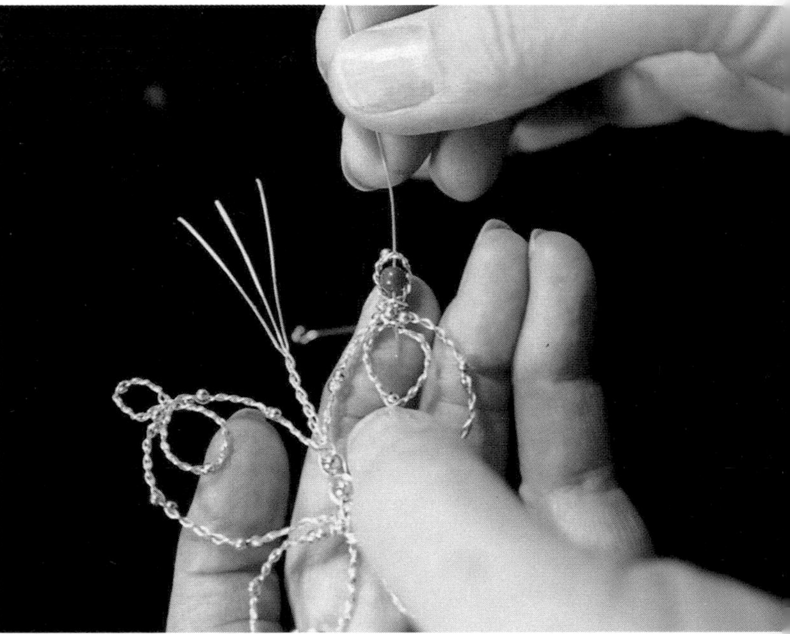

Cut a long piece of beading wire (5 inches) and push it through the frame, through the round stone bead, and out into the larger oval stone frame. Crimp and tuck the end that sticks out at the top of the wing.

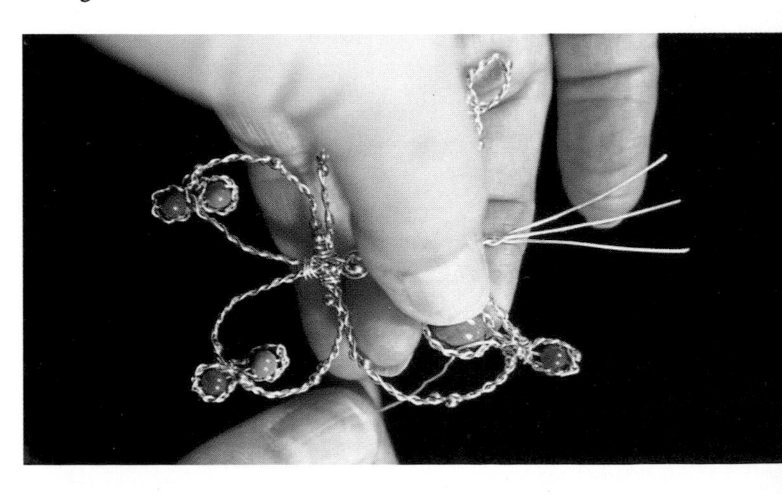

Next, with the flat-backed stone in place, run the retaining wire from the top through an opening in the side of the large stone frame. This will make a loop running from 12 o'clock to almost 3 o'clock, your first front retainer.

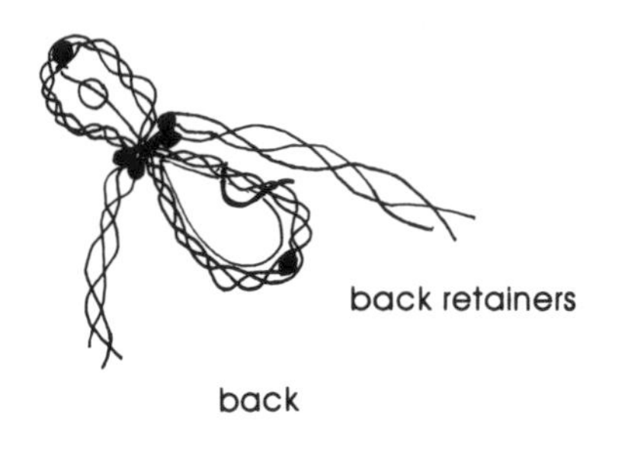

Looking at the *back* of the butterfly, re-insert the retaining wire slightly after the 3 o'clock point to make a back retainer.

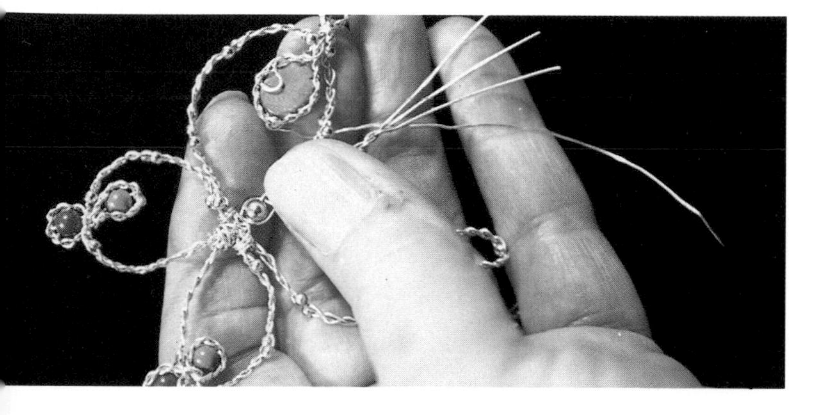

The back of the butterfly should now look like this.

Now run the retaining wire down to the bottom of the stone frame. This will make your second front retainer.

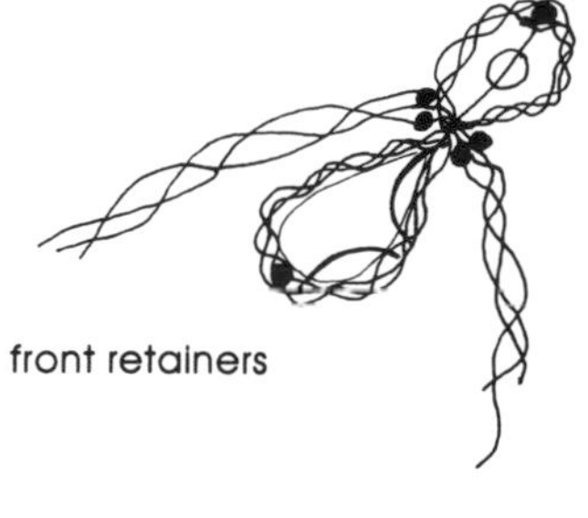

Insert it slightly before the 6 o'clock point, to allow room on the back for a back retainer.

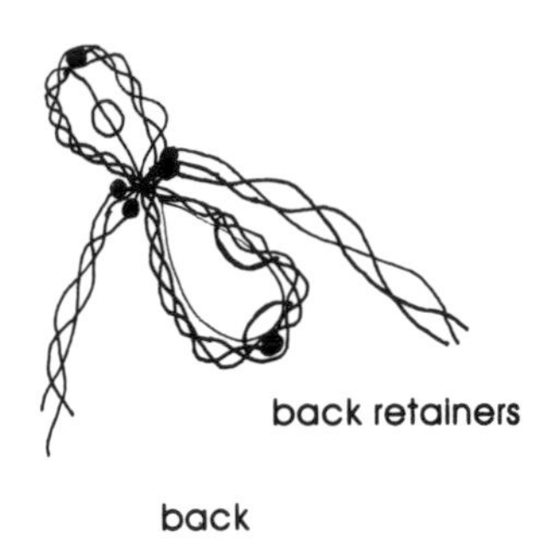

Re-insert the wire just after the 6 o'clock point to make the second back retainer.

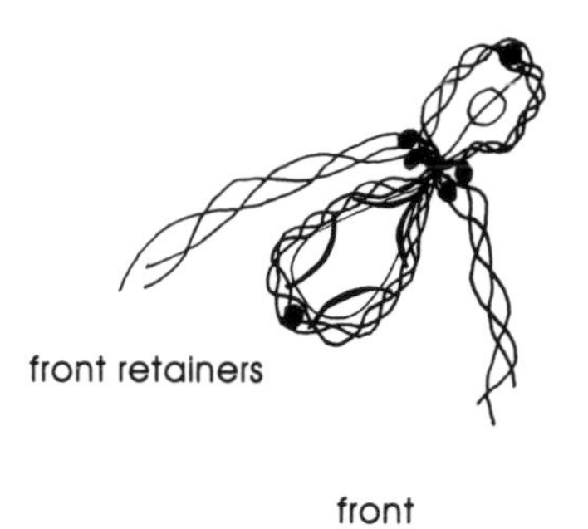

Continue like this around the rest of the loop, cutting and tucking the final end.

The front of the finished stone frame should look like this, with four front retainers holding the stone in place.

Here is the back view, with three back retainers. Repeat these steps for the loops on the second wing, and you will be ready to finish off your butterfly!

Making the Chain Loop

To make the chain loop at the top of the butterfly, bend it over a nail or something round.

Pass the center wire through an opening in the lowest braid in the Chain Loop. Pull the wire through until it is tight, wrap it around the base of the loop, cut it, and tuck in the end.

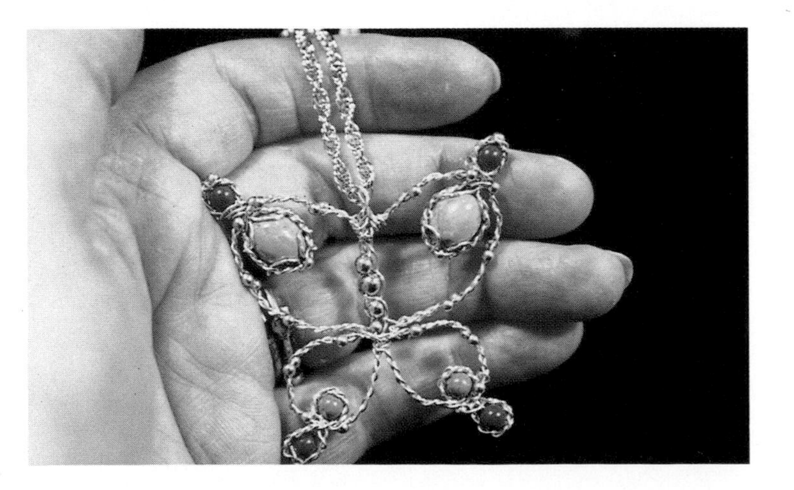

Wrap one of the outside wires around each wing next to the chain loop (two wraps each), cut them, and tuck the ends out of sight. The front should look like this.

Here is the back. Mix epoxy glue and lightly coat the back of the stones and the retaining wires. Your butterfly pendant is completed!

Making Pins & Earrings

To make dangling earrings, make the project exactly as if you were making a hanging pendant (above), and then add fishhook earring mounts through the chain loops. If you are making post earrings, clip earrings, or pins, you will need to start your project in a slightly different way: after you tape your three 13 inch wires together at the top, make only two tight, plain braids instead of the eight necessary for a chain loop. If you've already made the eight plain braids at the top and you change your mind about what type of jewelry you'd like to make, simply cut the braid about 1/4 inch above the body beads. Cut and tuck the ends of the two-braid top segment back into the body of the butterfly. Then glue your pinback, clip, or post to the butterfly. Be sure when you are making a pin that the hinge of the pin is at the top (head) of the butterfly.

DEFINITIONS:
MATERIALS, TOOLS, & TERMINOLOGY

BEADING WIRE- Any thin wire used to string beads by passing the wire through the bead openings.

BRAID- When three wires are laying side-by-side or are taped together, one outside wire is bent over the center wire (thus becoming the new center wire); then the outside wire on the other side is bent over the center wire. This makes one complete braid.

CENTER WIRE- In a braid, the wire between the two outside wires.

CHAIN LOOP- The unbeaded portion of the braided wire that is used to form a loop for a neckchain to pass through.

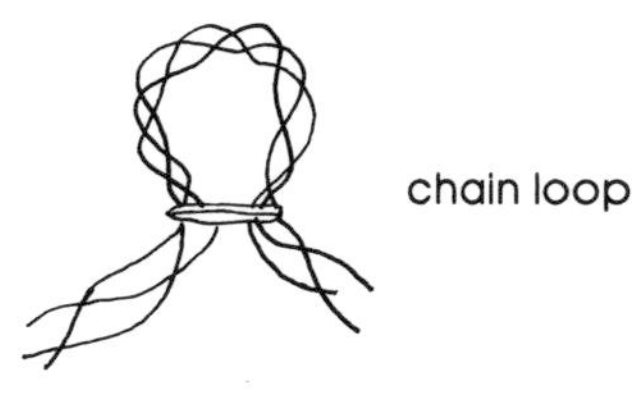

CRIMP- A bend at the very end of a wire to form a hook.

crimp

CRISS CROSS- Interweaving the three loose wires at the end of one braid with three loose wires at the end of another braid.

EPOXY GLUE- A strong, fast-setting glue consisting of two parts, the resin and the hardener.

FLAT-BACKED STONES- Round or oval stones with flat back surfaces and flat or domed front surfaces.

FRAME BEADS- beads that are put on the frame wires while braiding.

HALF-BRAID- When working with a braid or three side-by-side wires, one outside wire bent over the center wire (thus becoming the new center wire). A half-braid is used when there's a need to change the placement of the frame beads or to add length to the frame to compensate for length that has been take up by a joint (fig. D-11).

HALF-HITCH KNOT- Pushing the wire through an opening in a braid, and back out through another opening, winding the wire back through the loop you just made.

HIGH WIRE- The last wire bent into the center of a braid.

HOOK- A bend in a piece of wire that is used to catch hold of another piece of wire. For a single wire, this is made with a crimp; on a larger scale (like the fastener of the watchband) a braided hook can be made by bending a braided loop with the pliers.

HOOK LOOP- A braided loop used in conjunction with a braided hook (see HOOK) to form a closure for a piece of jewelry.

JOINT- Where two or more sections of a wire frame come together.

LOW WIRE- The first wire bent into the center of a braid, over which the HIGH WIRE crosses.

OUTSIDE WIRES- The wires that are on the right and the left of the center wire in a braid.

RETAINING WIRES or RETAINERS- Wires placed in such a way that they hold a stone or a bead in its mounting.

SMOOTH-JAWED NEEDLE-NOSE PLIERS- A pair of pliers that are tapered to a point and that do not have serrated jaws for gripping.

TUCK- To fold the edges of wires under another wire in the frame to make the wire secure.

WRAP- To wind or fold a piece of wire around the area designated in the pattern, to add strength and and give a finished look.

BEADING PATTERNS

CENTER WIRE FRAME BEADS- A beading pattern in which framing beads are placed on the center wire of the braided frame (see pp. 50-51).

DOUBLE-SIDED FRAME BEADS- A beading pattern in which frame beads are threaded onto both outside wires of a braid (see pp. 19-20).

DIAGONAL FRAME BEADS- A beading pattern in which frame beads are added to a braid as follows: put one bead on an outside wire and bend that wire over the center wire. Place a bead on the center wire, and bend the other outside wire over it. Bend the wire on the side where you started over the center wire. Then put a frame bead on the opposite outside wire and bend it over the center wire (see p. 6).

DIAMOND FRAME BEADS- A beading pattern in which frame beads are added to a braid as follows: put one bead on the center wire and one on the high outside wire. Bend the low outside wire over the center wire. Bend the high outside wire over the center wire. Put a bead on the low outside wire and the center wire, bend the low wire over the center wire, then the high outside wire over the center wire.

ONE SIDED FRAME BEADS- A beading pattern in which all the frame beads are placed on one side of the braided wire frame.

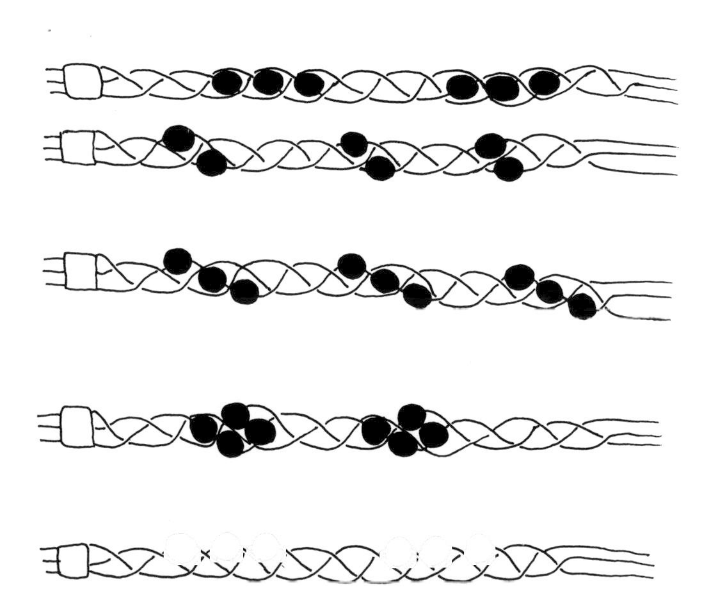

A Partial List of Suppliers

There are hundreds of lapidary shops, rock shops, and bead suppliers across the United States. Many of them sell a complete line of tools, gemstones, and beads and wires. You can find some of them by reading *Lapidary Magazine* and *Rock and Gem Magazine*, which have advertisements for many suppliers in addition to some very good articles. The New Mexico Jewelers Association (P.O. Box 3896, Albuquerque, NM 87190, (505) 292-0302) distributes a book entitled *Jewelry Goods and Services Sources Directory*, which can be obtained free of charge.

The following list is not meant as an endorsement of all of these shops, except those I have dealt with personally (marked with an asterisk).

* Arizona Minerals & Gems, Inc.
6370 East Hwy. 69
Prescott Valley, AZ 86314
(602)-772-6443
1-(800)-356-6903 for orders only
Fax (602)-772-1602

* Lone Star Rock Shop
2700 Holiday
Witchita Falls, TX

* V-Rock Shop
4760 Portage St. N.W.
North Canton, OH 44720
(216)-494-1759
1-(800)-458-7625
Fax (216)494-1432

M. Nowotny & Co.
8823 Callaghan Rd.
San Antonio, TX 78230
(210)-342-2512
1-(800)-950-8276

Pioneer Gem Corporation
P.O. Box 1513
Auburn, WA 98071
(206)-833-2760
1-(800)-433-9590

B & J Rock Shop
14744 Manchester Rd.
Ballwin, MO 63011
(315)-394-4567
Fax (314)394-7109

Gem-Fare
P.O. Box 213
Pittstown, NJ 08867
Fax (908)-806-3339

Ebersole Lapidary Supply Inc.
11417 West Hwy 54
Wichita, KS 67209-1298
(316)-722-4771

Abeda Corporation
1205 North Main Street
Royal Oak, MI 48067
(810)-399-6642
1-(800)-399-6642
Fax (810)-339-1920

Alpha Imports NY Inc.
2 West 46th St., Suite 1400
New York, NY 10036
(212)-575-2637
1-(800)-56alpha for orders only
Fax (212)-768-0599

Bead World
4931 Prospect N.E.
Albuquerque, NM 87110
(505)-884-3133
Fax (505)-884-7712

K&K International
P.O. Box 8172
Falls Ch., VA 22041
(703)-845-1686
1-(800)-92-9838
Fax (703)-931-3424

Richardson's Recreational Ranch
Gateway Route Box 440
Madras, OR 97741
(503)-475-2680

South Pacific Wholesale
Route 2, Box 249
E. Montpelier, VT 05651
1-(800)-338-2162
Fax 1-(800)-223-4044

Grieger's Inc.
Box 93070-26
Pasadena, CA 91109

Reflections by Lynn
23347 W. Lincoln Hwy
Plainfield, IL 60544
(815)-436-7952
Fax (815)-436-6393

*Betty's Bead Bank
300 W. Juneau
Milwaukee, WI 53203
(414)-276-8996

B. Rush Apple Company Fax.
3855 W. Kennedy Blvd.
Tampa, FL 33609
(813)-870-3180
Fax (813)-870-3183

Ron Larrivee
569 Main Street
Lewiston, ME 04240
(207)-782-0279

The Rock Peddler
58 Wedgewood Rd.
Franklin, NC 28734
Tel./fax (704)-524-6042

Heaven & Earth
RR1, Box 25
Marshfield, VT 05658

The Craft Market
401 5th Ave.
Fairbanks, AL 99701
(907)-452-5495

Maglinger Arts & Crafts
1328 W. 4th Street
Owensboro, KY 42301
(502)-683-514